RECOLLECTIONS AND EXPERIENCES

OF

AN ABOLITIONIST.

" Remember them in bonds."

RECOLLECTIONS AND EXPERIENCES

OF

AN ABOLITIONIST;

FROM 1855 TO 1865.

ALEXANDER MILTON ROSS

———

"Whatsoever ye would that man should do to you, do you even so to them."—MATT. vii. 12.

NEW FOREWORD BY DONALD FRANKLIN JOYCE

METRO BOOKS, INC.
Northbrook, Ill.
1972

Copyright © 1972 by Metro Books, Inc.

Library of Congress Catalog Card Number 77-99403

Standard Book Number 0-8411-0074-8

The original edition of this work was published in
Toronto in 1875 by Rowsell and Hutchinson. The
copy from which this reprint edition was made was
loaned to Metro Books, Inc. from the Vivian G. Harsh
Collection of Afro-American History and Literature,
George Cleveland Hall Branch, The Chicago Public
Library.

Manufactured in the United States

91744

FOREWORD

AT the close of the Civil War, there were between forty and fifty thousand Black people who lived in Canada. Aided by American and Canadian abolitionists, many of these Black people were fugitive slaves who had escaped to Canada from the claws of United States slavery. Prominent among the most active Canadian abolitionists was Dr. Alexander Milton Ross, a physician and ornithologist. Fired into action after reading Harriet Beecher Stowe's UNCLE TOM'S CABIN, Ross left his native Toronto in late 1856 for the "Land of Bondage" where he hoped to aid slaves make their escape to the freedom of Canada.

Stopping in New York and Philadelphia for several months to obtain advice and counsel from prominent and seasoned abolitionists, Ross arrived in Richmond, Virginia, in April, 1857, ready to begin his dangerous behind-the-scenes work of training and equipping slaves

FOREWORD

for the escape North to freedom in Canada.
Using letters of introduction from northern
abolitionists to anti-slavery sympathizers in
Richmond, Ross arranged several secret meetings with slaves from plantations around the
city. After ascertaining the depth of the determination and willingness of a selected number
of slaves to make the perilous trip to Canada.
Ross drilled them on routes and methods of
travel which would be necessary to elude their
possible captors. One night, after his arrival in
Richmond, nine men, equipped with food,
money, and pistols supplied by him, quietly left
the city on the hazardous journey to Canada.

Using the same plan of action, Ross sent
slaves to Canada from Memphis, Tennessee,
New Orleans, Louisiana, Augusta, Georgia,
Huntsville, Alabama, Louisville, Kentucky, and
some rural community in Mississippi. His ven-
ture into Mississippi almost cost him his life.

A close personal friend of John Brown, Ross
records in these pages conversations and letters
between the martyred abolitionist and himself.
After learning of the date of Brown's planned
raid on Harper's Ferry, Ross repaired to Richmond to await the result of the raid.

"Soon after the reception of the above
letter I left for Richmond, Virginia, much

against the wishes of my friends. I had promised Captain Brown, during our interview at Springfield, Massachusetts, that when he was ready to make his attack on the Slave States, I would go to Richmond and await the result."

Before John Brown's execution, Ross made a personal appeal to Governor Wise of Virginia to see the prisoner. In an interview with the Governor, Ross' request was rejected with a threat of death if he made any attempt to see Brown.

"I am wise enough to understand your object in wishing to go to Charlestown, and I dare you to go. If you attempt it, I will have you shot."

During the Civil War, Ross was commissioned personally by President Lincoln to be a serveillant to Confederate activities in Canada reporting directly to him. Ross successfully exposed and crushed the Confederate foreign mail service which was secretly being routed through Canada, and apprehended a Confederate officer who was enroute to New Brunswick to plan a Conferedate invasion of Union territory from Canada.

FOREWORD

This first-person narrative by one of the most daring abolitionists gives an intimate view of the field activities of the men who believed in freedom for the Black slaves. With speeches, private conversations, and letters by the leaders of the movement, RECOLLECTIONS AND EXPERIENCES OF AN ABOLITIONIST uncovers many little known facts about the intrigues experienced by the abolitionists.

Donald Franklin Joyce, Curator
Vivian G. Harsh Collection of
Afro-American History and Literature,
George Cleveland Hall Branch
The Chicago Public Library
Chicago
1972

THIS VOLUME

OF

RECOLLECTIONS AND EXPERIENCES

IS, WITH SENTIMENTS OF PROFOUND HOMAGE AND RESPECT,
DEDICATED TO

HIS IMPERIAL MAJESTY

ALEXANDER II.

EMPEROR AND AUTOCRAT OF ALL THE
RUSSIAS,

WHO, OF HIS OWN SOVEREIGN WILL AND PLEASURE, GAVE
FREEDOM TO

TWENTY MILLIONS OF SERFS

OF THE RUSSIAN EMPIRE.

Toronto, May 1875.

PREFACE.

———

THESE Recollections and Experiences are given to the public in compliance with the repeated solicitations of many of my coloured friends, some of whom were personally interested in the experiences herein recorded.

In the preparation of this narrative, I have strictly refrained from any attempt at embellishment or amplification, and I have aimed at accuracy of statement, briefness of description, and simplicity of style.

A. M. R.

Toronto, May, 1875.

CONTENTS.

RECOLLECTIONS AND EXPERIENCES

OF

AN ABOLITIONIST.

——o——

CHAPTER I.

FIRST IMPRESSIONS OF HUMAN SLAVERY.

Y first impressions of human slavery were derived from the published speeches and writings of Wilberforce, Brougham, and other English abolitionists, which I read in my youth, and in later years from the eloquent appeals for the freedom of the enslaved, made by Wendell Phillips, William Lloyd Garrison, Theodore Parker, and Gerrit Smith. The impulses gained from the above sources excited my sympathies, and impelled me to seek for further and more practical information as to the workings of the institution of slavery in the

1

American Republic. I had not far to seek for
the desired knowledge, for there were in Canada
hundreds of escaped slaves, living witnesses to
the hideous barbarity of that wicked institution.
From them I heard heart-rending stories of the
cruelties practised upon the poor oppressed
coloured people of the Slave States. In proof
of their statements I was shown the indelible
marks of the lash and branding-iron upon their
bodies.

These refugees were, as a general rule, superior
specimens of their race, and possessed qualities,
in the majority of cases, which fitted them for
all the duties of citizenship. Many of those I
conversed with were quite intelligent, having
held positions as coachmen, house servants, and
body servants to their masters, and the information I obtained from them enabled me, in after
years, to render some service to their friends
in bondage.

UNCLE TOM'S CABIN.

While I was engaged in my inquiries among
the coloured people of Canada, Mrs. Stowe's
work, " Uncle Tom's Cabin," was published, and
excited the sympathies of every humane person
who read it, in behalf of the oppressed. To me

it was a command ; and a settled conviction took
possession of my mind, that it was my duty to
help the oppressed to freedom, to "remember
them in bonds, as bound with them." My resolution was taken, to devote all the energies of
my life to "let the oppressed go free."

I had learned from the refugees in Canada
that there existed in the Northern States relief
organizations, formed for the purpose of extending aid to fugitives from bondage. I also gathered from the same sources much information
relative to the various secret routes leading
from the Slave States to Canada, as well as the
names and addresses of many good friends of
freedom in the States of Ohio, Pennsylvania,
and Michigan, who cheerfully gave shelter and
aid to the escaped slaves whose objective point
was Canada—the Land of Liberty for the slaves
of the American Republic.

PREPARATION FOR THE WORK.

In November, 1856, I left Canada to prepare
for the work which had absorbed my thoughts for
years. A prominent abolitionist of Northern
New York had invited me to visit his home, and
confer with him in respect to the best way of
accomplishing the most good for the cause we

both had at heart. From this noble philanthropist and true Christian I obtained most valuable and interesting information as to the workings of the different organizations having for their object the liberation from bondage of the slaves of the South. He accompanied me to Boston, New York, and Philadelphia. I was introduced to many liberty-loving men and women, whose time, talents, and means, were devoted to the cause of freedom. The contact with such noble, enthusiastic minds, imbued with an undying hatred and detestation of that foul blot on the escutcheon of their country, served to strengthen my resolution and fortify me for the labour before me. I was initiated into a knowledge of the relief societies, and the methods adopted to circulate information among the slaves of the South; the routes to be taken by the slaves, after reaching the so-called Free States; the relief posts, where shelter and aid for transportation could be obtained.

The poor fugitive who had run the gauntlet of slave-hunters and blood-hounds was not safe, even after he had crossed the boundary line between the Slave and Free States, for the slave-drivers of the South and their allies, the democrats of the North, held control of the United States Government at that time; and under the provisions of the iniquitous "Fugitive Slave Law," the North was compelled to act as a police detective for the capture and return to slavery of the fugitives from the Slave States.

My excellent friend also accompanied me to Ohio and Indiana, where I made the personal acquaintance of friends in those States who, at risk of life and property, gave shelter to the fugitives, and assisted them in reaching Canada.

READY FOR THE WORK.

On my return to Philadelphia I made the necessary preparations for work in the Southern States.

In undertaking this enterprise I did not disguise from myself the dangers I would most certainly have to encounter, and the certainty that a speedy, and perhaps cruel, death would be my lot, in case my plans and purposes were discovered. And not only would my own life be exposed, but also the lives of those I sought to aid.

My kind friends in Boston and Philadelphia had warned me of the dangers that were in my path; and many of them urged me to seek other and less dangerous channels wherein to aid the oppressed. I felt convinced, however, that the only effectual way to help the slaves was, to aid them in escaping from bondage. To accomplish that, it was necessary to go to them, advise them, and give them practical assistance. With a few exceptions the negroes were in absolute ignorance of every thing beyond the boundary of their plantation or town.

The circulation of information among the slaves would also have a certain tendency to create a feeling of independence in the minds of the negroes, which, ultimately, would lead to insurrection, and perhaps the destruction of the institution of slavery.

At length all my preparations were completed, and I was ready to enter the land of bondage, and discharge, to the best of my ability, the duty that rested upon me.

Two years had passed since I had finished reading Mrs. Stowe's work, and the resolution which I then made, to devote my energies to "let the oppressed go free," was still fresh and strong.

Before leaving Philadelphia a mutual understanding was arranged between my friends and myself in respect to confidential correspondence, by which it was understood that the term "hardware," was to mean males; and "dry-goods," females. I was to notify my friends in Philadelphia (if possible) whenever a package of "hardware" or "dry-goods" was started for freedom; and they in turn warned the friends in Ohio and Pennsylvania to be on the look-out for runaways.

INTO THE LAND OF BONDAGE.

On a beautiful morning in April, 1857, I crossed the Potomac *en route* for Richmond. My outfit was compact, and contained in a small valise. The only weapon I had, was a small revolver, which had been presented to me by a Bostonian, who, in after years, honoured the office of Governor of Massachusetts.

On arriving in Richmond I went to the house of a gentleman to whom I had been directed, and who was known in the North to be a friend to the slaves. I spent a few weeks in quietly looking around, and determining upon the best plans to adopt.

THE WORK BEGINS.

Having finally decided upon my course, I invited a number of the most intelligent, active, and reliable slaves, to meet me at the house of a coloured preacher, on a Sunday evening.

On the night appointed for this meeting forty-two slaves came to hear what prospect there was for their escape from bondage. I shook each by the hand, asked their name, age, and whether married or single. I had never before seen, at one time, so many coloured men together, and I was struck with their individuality and general kindness and consideration for each other. I then explained to them my object and purposes in visiting the Slave States. I also carefully explained to them the various routes from Virginia to Ohio and Pennsylvania, and the names of friends in border towns who would help them on to Canada. I requested them to circulate this information discreetly among all upon whom they could rely. Thus, each of my hearers became an agent in the good work. I then told them that if any of their number chose to make the attempt to gain their freedom, in the face of all the obstacles and dangers in their path, that I would supply them with weapons to defend themselves, in case any attempt was made to deprive them of their right to freedom; and also, as much food as they could conveniently carry. I requested as many as were ready to accept my offer, to come to the same house on the following Sunday evening.

NINE FUGITIVES FROM BONDAGE.

On the evening appointed nine stout, intelligent young men had declared their determination to gain their freedom, or die in the attempt. To each I gave a few dollars in money, a pocket compass, a knife, and as much cold meat and bread as each could carry with ease. I again carefully explained to them the route, and the names of friends along the border upon whom they could rely for shelter and assistance. I never met more apt students than these poor fellows ; and their " Yes, massa, I know it now," was assurance that they did. They were to travel only by night, resting in some secure spot during the day. Their route was to be through Pennsylvania to Erie, on Lake Erie, and from thence to Canada. I bid them good bye with an anxious heart, for well I knew the dangers they had to encounter. I learned many months after that they all arrived safely in Canada. (In 1863, I enlisted three of these brave fellows in a coloured regiment in Philadelphia, for service in the war that gave freedom to their race). Two of my Richmond pupils were married men, and left behind them wives and children. The wife of one made her escape, and reached Canada within six months after her husband gained his liberty. (I visited their happy little home, in Chatham, Canada, in after years, and was delighted to find them prosperous and contented).

AT WORK AGAIN.

The day following the departure of my little band of fugitives from Richmond, I left for Nashville, in the State of Tennessee, which I decided should be my next field of labour. On my arrival in Nashville I went direct to the residence of a Quaker lady, well known for her humane and charitable disposition toward the coloured people. When I informed her of my success in Richmond, and that I intended to pursue the same course in Nashville, she expressed great anxiety for my safety. But finding that I was determined to make the attempt, she sent for an old free negro, and advised me to trust him implicitly. This good man was nearly eighty years of age, and had the confidence of all the coloured people for miles around Nashville. He lived a short distance outside the city limits. At his house he preached to such of the slaves as were disposed and could attend, every Sunday evening. I requested him to invite as many of the most reliable and intelligent of the slaves as he could to meet me at his house on the next Sunday evening.

On the evening appointed I found thirteen

fine able-bodied men assembled to see and hear
an abolitionist. Seldom have I seen a finer or
more intelligent looking lot of coloured men
than those that composed my little audience on
that occasion; their ages ranged from 18 to 30.
Some of them were very black, while others
were mulattoes, and two of them had straight
hair, and were very light-coloured; but all
of them had an earnest and intelligent look.
My host volunteered to stand guard outside the house, to prevent interruption and to
intercept any friendly or evil minded callers.
I talked to my hearers earnestly and practically
for two hours, explaining the condition and
prospects of the coloured people in Canada, the
obstacles and dangers they would have to
encounter, the route to be taken, and the names
of friends, north of the Ohio river, to whom they
could safely apply for aid to help them on to
Canada. No lecturer ever had a more intensely
earnest audience than I had that evening. I
gathered them close around me, so that I could
look each in the face, and give emphasis to my
instructions. In conclusion, I told them that I
should remain in Nashville until after the following Sunday evening, when as many as felt
disposed to make the attempt to gain their freedom could meet me in the same house at 9 p.m.
I requested those who would decide to leave

on that night to inform their old friend before the next Friday, that I might make some provision for their long and perilous journey.

Early in the week I received word from five; and by Friday evening two more had decided to make the attempt to obtain liberty.

At 9 o'clock, on the Sunday evening appointed, I was promptly at the house of my friend. He again stood guard. It was nearly 10 o'clock before I heard the signal agreed upon —"scratching upon the door." I unlocked the door, when in stepped four men, followed soon after by three others. They were all young men and unmarried. I asked each if he had fully determined to make the attempt; and receiving an affirmative reply, I very carefully explained to them the routes to be taken, the dangers they might expect to encounter, and the friends upon whom they could call for aid. To each I gave a pistol, a knife, a pair of shoes, a compass, and to their leader twenty dollars in money. They were also supplied with as much food as they could conveniently carry.

SEVEN CANDIDATES FOR FREEDOM.

At midnight I bid them good-bye; and these brave-hearted fellows, with tears in their eyes, and hearts swelling with thankfulness toward me, started for the land of freedom. I advised them to travel by night only, to keep together, and not use their pistols except in absolute necessity.

Next morning I called upon my Quaker friend and informed her of the result of my labours in Nashville. She expressed her delight and satis-faction ; but feared for my safety, if I remained in the city after the escape of the slaves became known.

That evening I sent letters to friends in Evansville, Cincinnati, and Cleveland, to keep a sharp lookout for " packages of hardware."

As I was leaving the Post Office a man handed me a small printed bill, which an-nounced the escape of thirteen slaves from Richmond ; but nine only were described, toge-ther with the names of their owners. A reward of $1,000 was offered for their capture and return to Richmond. I now thought it was time for me to leave for other fields of labour. Early next day I bade farewell to my kind Quaker friend, and started for Memphis. On my arrival there I sought the house of an anti-slavery man to whom I had been directed. The husband was absent from home, but the good

wife received me most kindly, and urged me to
make her house my home during my stay in the
city. I felt, however, that I had no right to
expose the family to trouble and suspicion, in
case I got into difficulty. I went to a hotel,
and being tired and weary, laid down upon a
couch to rest, and must have fallen asleep, for I
was aroused by the shouting of a newsboy under
my window. The burthen of his cry was, the
escape of several slaves from Nashville in one
night. I opened the window, and told the boy
to bring a paper up to my room. The news
was as follows :—

TWELVE HUNDRED DOLLARS REWARD.

"Great excitement in Nashville—Escape of
seven first-class slave-men, by the aid of an
abolitionist who had been seen prowling about
the city for several days previous." Three hundred dollars reward was offered for the capture
and return of each of the slaves, and twelve
hundred dollars for the apprehension of the
"accursed" abolitionist ; then followed a description of the slaves, and a very good description
of myself, considering that I had kept very close
during my stay in Nashville. At a glance I saw
the danger of my position, and determined to
leave the hotel at once, which I did ; returning
to the house I had first visited, I told the good

wife my position. The paper, which contained the exciting news, also contained the announcement that a steamer would leave for St. Louis that night at nine o'clock. It was now three. Six long hours to remain in the very jaws of death! I made enquiries for the house of a coloured man, upon whom my old coloured friend in Nashville told me I could rely. Having received the proper direction, I went to his humble dwelling, and mentioning the name of his old friend at Nashville, he cordially welcomed me. He was a fine looking man, with honest eyes, open countenance, and of more than ordinary intelligence, for one of his race. I handed him the paper, and pointed to the reward for my apprehension. When he read the exciting news, he grasped my hand and said, " Massa, I'd die to save you ; what shall we do ?" I told him I had determined to leave by nine o'clock that night, if possible, on the steamboat for St. Louis, and asked permission to remain in his house until the arrival of the steamer. The noble fellow placed his house, and all he possessed at my command. On many occasions I have placed my life in the hands of coloured men without the slightest hesitation or fear of betrayal.

A POOR NEGRO SPURNS THE REWARD.

This poor despised negro held in his hand a
a paper offering a reward of $1,200 for my cap-
ture.   He was a labouring man, earning his
bread by the sweat of his brow ; and yet I felt
perfectly safe, and implicitly trusted this poor
man with my life.   In fact, I felt safer in his house
than I should have felt in the house of a certain
Vice-President of the U. S., who, in more recent
times sold himself for a similar amount.   This
poor oppressed negro, had everything to gain by
surrendering me into the hands of the slave-
masters, and yet he spurned the reward, and
was faithful to the trust I had placed in him.

Night was now approaching, and my friend
suggested the propriety of shaving off my whis-
kers and changing my dress.   While engaged
making these alterations I overheard an animated
conversation, in the adjoining room, between my
host and a female.   The woman earnestly begged of him to ask me to take her to Canada,
where her husband then was.   The poor man told
her my life was already in great danger, and that
I might be captured and killed, if she .was
seen with me ; but still she continued to beg.
When I had completed my change of appearance, he came into the room, and told me

that in the next room was a coloured woman that had lately fled from her master on account of his cruelty to her. I told him to bring her in, and let me talk with her. She was about thirty-five years old, and a light mulatto, of bright, intelligent appearance. She told me of the escape of her husband to Canada about two years previously, and of her master's cruelty in beating her, because she refused to marry a negro whom he had selected for her. She showed me her back, which was still raw and seamed with deep gashes, where the lash of her cruel master's whip had ploughed up her flesh. She earnestly implored me to take her to Canada. I told my friend to dress her in male attire, so that she might accompany me in the capacity of *valet*, and that I would make the attempt to take her to Canada. The poor creature gladly accepted the offer, and was soon ready for the journey. I gave her the name of " Sam," and myself the title of " Mr. Smith, of Kentucky." At half-past eight, p.m., we left the house of my faithful friend, and started for the boat, " Sam" walking behind me, carrying my valise. Through some cause or other the boat was detained until near eleven o'clock. Oh, what hours of misery! every minute filled with apprehensions of disaster, not only to myself, but to the poor creature depending upon me. No one, not similarly

2

placed, can imagine the anxiety and dread that filled my mind during this long delay. The moments passed so slowly, that they seemed hours. "Sam" stood near me, looking as anxious as I felt. At length we got aboard the boat. I secured tickets for myself and servant for St. Louis, and when the boat left the levee, I breathed freer than I had for several hours.

I arrived in St. Louis without the occurrence of any incident of importance, and sent telegrams to different points along the Ohio river to friends, warning them to be on the lookout for fugitives from Tennessee. I remained in St. Louis but a few hours, and left for Chicago, accompanied by my happy servant, whose frequent question, "Massa, is we near Canada yet," kept me continually on the alert to prevent her from exposing herself to arrest.

ARRIVAL IN CHICAGO WITH A CHATTEL.

When we reached Chicago, I took my servant to the house of a friend of the slave, where she was properly cared for. It was deemed prudent, however, that she should continue to wear male attire until she reached Canada, for it occasionally occurred that fugitives were caught in Detroit, and taken back to bondage,

after having come in sight of the land of promise. Their proximity to a safe refuge from their
taskmasters, and from the operation of the infamous Fugitive Slave Law, rendered them careless
in their manner, and so happy in appearance,
that they were frequently arrested on suspicion
by the minions of the United States Government,
ever on the watch to obey the behests of the
slave power. After a few hours' rest in Chicago,
I left with my charge for Detroit, where I arrived
in due time on the following day ; and, taking
a hack, drove to a friend's house in the suburbs
of the city. Here I made arrangements to be
rowed across the river to Windsor, Canada, in
a small boat, as soon as darkness would render
our passage safe. I also sent telegrams to friends
in London, Chatham, and Amherstburg, to ascertain the whereabouts of her husband, and finally
heard that he was working in a barber shop in
London.

SAFE ON THE SOIL OF CANADA.

At night the poor fugitive and myself were
taken silently over the river that separated the
land of freedom from the land of slavery. Not
a word was spoken until we touched the soil of
Canada. I then told her that she was now a
free woman, and no one could now deprive her of

her right to " life, liberty, and the pursuit of happiness." She dropped on her knees, and uttered
a sincere prayer to the Almighty to protect and
bless me for bringing her to Canada. I took her
to the house of a friend, and on the following day
sent her to London, where she and her husband
were united, after a separation of two years.
(In 1863 I dined with them at their pretty little
home, which they had paid for with the proceeds
of their industry and thrift). Returning to Detroit I took the cars for Cleveland. On my
arrival there I received a telegram from Boston
informing me that Capt. John Brown, of Kansas,
would meet me in Cleveland in a day or two,
and that he desired to confer with me on a
subject of importance, connected with the Anti-
slavery cause.

FIRST INTERVIEW WITH JOHN BROWN.

On the evening of my third day in Cleveland,
while seated in my room at the hotel, a gentle
tap at my door aroused me ; I said, " come in "
(thinking it was a servant) ; the door opened,
and in walked a plain, farmer-like looking man
—a stranger, but with a remarkable countenance,
strongly indicative of intelligence, coolness, tenacity of purpose, and honesty. He appeared
about five feet ten inches in height, slender, but

wiry and tough ; his glance keen, steady, and honest ; his step light, quick, and firm. He was, although simply and plainly dressed, a man of remarkable appearance ; no close observer would pass him on the street without making that observation. He introduced himself as "John Brown, of Kansas," and handed me several letters from friends in Boston and Philadelphia.

While I was engaged reading the letters, and occasionally asking a question in reference to their contents, he was closely examining a revolver of mine which he had found on my bureau. When I had finished reading the letters he remarked, "How very strange that you should have a pistol exactly like one I have in my pocket," which he produced. They were, indeed, fellows in every respect, and presented to us by the same generous Bostonian. Capt. Brown remained with me until after midnight, eagerly listening to a narrative of my trip through Virginia and Tennessee, and in relating incidents connected with his labours in Kansas. His manner and conversation produced a magnetic influence which rendered him very attractive, and stamped him as a man of more than ordinary coolness, tenacity of purpose, and devotion to what he considered right. He was, in my estimation, a Christian in the full sense of that word.

No idle, profane, or immodest word fell from his lips. He was deeply in earnest in the work, in which he believed himself a special instrument in the hands of God. During our long (and to me deeply interesting) interview, which lasted from 8 p.m. until 3 in the morning, he related many incidents of his life bearing upon the subject of slavery. He said he had for many years been studying the guerilla system of warfare adopted in the mountainous portions of Italy and Switzerland ; that he could, with a small body of picked men, inaugurate and maintain a negro insurrection in the mountains of Virginia, which would produce so much annoyance to the United States Government, and create such a feeling of dread and insecurity in the minds of slaveholders, that slavery would ultimately be abolished.

HIS OPINION OF ABOLITIONISTS.

Capt. Brown had little respect for that class of abolitionists who, from their abodes of safety in the North, spoke so bravely in behalf of the oppressed coloured people of the Slave States, but who took good care to keep their precious bodies north of the Potomac. He stoutly maintained that the only way to abolish slavery was by conveying to the slaves such information as would aid them in making their escape to Canada, and by encouraging insurrection among the slaves; thus producing feelings of dread and uncertainty in the minds of slaveholders, that would end in the emancipation of the slaves.

HIS DISAPPOINTMENTS.

John Brown was now returning to Kansas, from the Eastern States, where he had been for several weeks trying to collect means to carry on the war in Kansas. He said he had found by experience that those abolitionists who made the most noise from the pulpits and lecture-rooms, were the last to offer a dollar toward any practical means for the liberation of the slaves. He had met with disappointment in the East, and felt it most keenly. He had sacrificed his own peace and comfort, and the peace and comfort of his family, in obedience to his sincere convictions of duty toward the oppressed people of the South, while those who had the means to help him make war upon the oppressor, were lukewarm or declined to aid him in his warfare.

CHARACTER OF JOHN BROWN.

I have been in the presence of many men whom the world called great and distinguished, but never before or since have I met a greater or more remarkable man than Capt. John Brown. There was manifest, in all he said and did, an absorbing intensity of purpose, controlled by lofty moral principles. He was a devout Christian ; and sincerely believed himself a chosen instrument in the hands of God to let the oppressed go free.

HE LEAVES FOR KANSAS.

Capt. Brown left me at an early hour in the morning, to take the cars for Kansas. Before parting I urged him to accept from me a portion of my funds, to aid him in the purchase of material for his Kansas work. This he did reluctantly, expressing his fears that I was depriving myself of the means to continue my labours.

CHAPTER II.

NEWS FROM THE SOUTH.

THE excitement in Richmond and Nashville, consequent upon the escape of so many valuable slaves, extended to all the surrounding country. In the reading room of the hotel at which I was stopping, I picked up a Richmond paper, which contained a lengthy account of the escape of slaves from Richmond, Nashville, and other parts of the South. The writer stated that a general impression prevailed in that community, that a regularly organized band of abolitionists existed in the South, which supplied the negroes with information and means to escape to Canada. The authorities were urged to offer a large reward for the apprehension of the "cursed negro thieves" that infested the South, and that an example should be made of such as were caught, as would for ever deter others from interference with the rights of the South.

KEEPING QUIET.

I concluded it would be better for the cause, I tried to serve, that no further attempt should be made until the present excitement in the South quieted down. From Cleveland I went to Philadelphia, where I remained until November, 1857. During my stay in that city I was busily occupied in collecting statistics of the slave populations of the different Slave States, and in consulting with various friends as to the best methods of circulating information among the slaves of the Cotton States.

Any one acquainted with the institution of slavery, as it existed in the Gulf States, will fully appreciate the difficulties that environed such an enterprise as 'the one I now contemplated—that of conveying direct to the slaves a knowledge of the best routes, the distances to be traversed, difficulties to be overcome, and the fact that they had friends in the Border States to whom they could apply for aid, and on whom they could implicitly rely for assistance to forward them to Canada. Of all the dangers to myself that loomed up before my mind, the last and the least was the fear of betrayal by the slaves. Once they became satisfied of your friendship and your desire to help them escape from bondage, they would willingly suffer torture or death to protect you. Such, at least, has been my experience with the negroes of the Slave States.

OFF FOR NEW ORLEANS.

Early in the month of December, 1857, I left New York, by steamer, for New Orleans, on a mission, the subject and details of which had occupied my mind exclusively for many months. I was accompanied to the steamer by two noble-hearted and steadfast friends of freedom. One of these friends (a resident of the interior of New York State) had been my principal supporter, and active and unflinching friend from the commencement of my career as an abolitionist. The other, was a resident of Brooklyn, a prominent philanthropist, long identified with the abolitionists of the North. All my correspondence, while in the Slave States, was to be sent to them. Whenever a slave succeeded in making his or her escape I was to send them the information, and they in turn notified our friends north of the Ohio river to be on the lookout for " packages of hardware" (men) or " dry goods" (females), and these Ohio friends concealed the fugitives for a time, if necessary, until they could be safely sent to Canada. In many parts of Ohio, Michigan, Indiana, and Pennsylvania, we had fast friends, in the majority of cases belonging to the Society of Quakers, whose doors were always open to the poor fugitive from bondage, and whose hearts were open to the fugitive's appeal for help.

ARRIVAL IN NEW ORLEANS.

On my arrival in New Orleans I secured board with a private family, and began my preparations for work in the interior of the country. From childhood I had been passionately fond of the study of Natural History, especially of Ornithology. I consequently decided to follow the pursuit of a naturalist, as a guise to my actual object.

SLAVE AUCTIONS.

During my stay in New Orleans I occasionally attended the slave auctions. The scenes I witnessed there will never be effaced from my memory. The horrid traffic in human beings, many of them much whiter and more intelligent than the cruel men who bought and sold them, was, without exception, the most monstrous outrage upon the rights of a human being that can possibly be conceived of. The cries and heart-rending agonies of the poor creatures as they were sold and separated from parents, children, husbands, or wives, will never cease to ring in my ears. Babes were torn from the arms of their mothers and sold, while parents were separated and sent to distant parts of the country. I have seen tired and overworked women cruelly beaten because they refused the outrageous demands of their wicked overseers.

HORRORS OF HUMAN SLAVERY.

My experience in New Orleans served to intensify my abhorrence and hatred toward that vile and unchristian institution of slavery, and to nerve me for the work I was engaged in. On several occasions I attended divine worship, and I invariably noticed that whenever the subject of slavery was mentioned, it was referred to as a "wise and beneficent institution"; and one clergyman in particular declared that "the institution of slavery was devised by God for the especial benefit of the coloured race."

Finally my preparations were completed, and, supplied with a shot gun, and materials for preserving bird-skins, I began my journey into the interior of the country.

The route I had decided upon was from New Orleans to Vicksburg, and thence through the interior of Mississippi, Alabama, Georgia, South Carolina, North Carolina, and Florida. I had never before visited that part of the United States, and my field of labour was consequently surrounded by difficulties not experienced during my visit to Virginia and Tennessee, from the fact that I had not a single friend in the Cotton States.

AT WORK NEAR VICKSBURG.

On my arrival at Vicksburg I obtained board in a private family, and was soon busily engaged in collecting ornithological specimens. I made frequent visits to the surrounding plantations, seizing every favourable opportunity to converse with the more intelligent of the slaves. Many of these negroes had heard of Canada from the negroes brought from Virginia, and the border Slave States; but the impression they had was, that Canada was so far away that it would be useless to try and reach it. I was usually accompanied on these excursions by one or two smart, intelligent slaves, to whom I felt I could trust the secret of my visit. In this way I succeeded in circulating a knowledge of Canada, and the best means of reaching that country, to all the plantations for many miles around Vicksburg. I was often surprised at the rapidity with which information was conveyed to the slaves of distant plantations. Thus, on every plantation I had missionaries who were secretly conveying the intelligence to the poor downtrodden slaves of that benighted region, that in Canada there were hundreds of negroes who had, through the aid of friends along the border, escaped from slavery, and were now free men and women.

No one but a slave can fully appreciate the true meaning of the word freedom.

I continued my labours in the vicinity of Vicksburg for two months, and then went to Selma, Ala.

SOWING SEED AT SELMA.

I made this place my base for extensive excursions to the surrounding country, pursuing a similar course to that I adopted at Vicksburg. My ornithological collection had by this time assumed respectable and interesting proportions, and some of the planters became so much interested in my apparent pursuit, as to offer me every facility to roam over their plantations, of which I availed myself. I had my choice of assistants from among the slaves, and selected those possessing qualities suitable for my purpose. There was not a plantation within fifteen miles of Selma that I did not visit successfully. The seed planted at Vicksburg and Selma fell upon rich soil, the products of which rapidly spread throughout the Gulf States, as was plainly evinced at the time of the Harper's Ferry invasion, when the planters in the interior of the South were surprised to find that their slaves were well informed about Canada, and the purposes and efforts of friends in the North to aid them in escaping from bondage.

IN A DANGEROUS POSITION.

Having completed my labours at Selma, I selected Columbus, Mississippi, for my next field of labour. I had been at work in Columbus about two weeks when a difficulty occurred which, but for the faithfulness of a negro, would have ended in my death at the hands of an infuriated mob. During one of my visits to a plantation near Columbus, I met with a negro slave of more than ordinary intelligence. His master was a man of coarse and brutal instincts, who had burned the initials of his name into the flesh of several of his slaves, to render their capture more certain in case they attempted to escape from this merciless wretch. I saw several of the victims of his cruelty, whose backs would forever bear the marks of his branding iron and lash. He was a veritable "Legree." On one of my excursions over his plantation I was accompanied by the slave mentioned. During our rambles he gave me a history of his life and sufferings, and expressed an earnest desire to gain his freedom. I felt that he could be relied upon, and imparted to him the secret object of my visit to the South. He listened with absorbing earnestness while I explained to him the difficulties and dangers he would have to encounter on so long and perilous a journey. He, however, declared his determination to make the attempt, saying, that death itself was preferable to his present existence. On the following day (Saturday) I again visited the plantation, and selected this slave for my companion. He informed me he had decided to start for Canada, as soon as he could communicate with a brother, who was a slave on a plantation a few miles distant. He wished to take this brother with him, if possible. I gave him instructions for his guidance after he should cross the Ohio river; the names of friends at Evansville (Ind.), and Cleveland (Ohio), to whom he could apply for assistance. I also furnished him with a pistol,

3

knife, and pocket compass, and directed him
to travel by night only until he reached friends
north of the Ohio river.

INTO THE JAWS OF DEATH.

On the following Monday evening, while
seated at the supper table of the hotel at which
I was stopping, I heard loud and excited talking
in the adjoining room. In a few minutes the
landlord came up to me with an excited look,
and said, "Col. ——— wishes to speak with
you. You had better go out and meet him."
I immediately rose, and went into the room
from which the loud talking emanated. As I
entered, the Colonel, in a loud and brutal tone,
said, "That's him, arrest him," Upon which a
man stepped up and said, "You are my prisoner."
I demanded the reason why I was arrested.
Whereupon the doughty Colonel strode toward
me with his fist clenched, and charged me with
being a d——d abolitionist; and said he would
have my heart's blood ; that I had enticed away
his nigger "Joe ;" that the nigger had not been
seen since he went out with me on the previous
Saturday.

The room was filled with an excited crowd
of men, who glared upon me with fierce and

fiendish looks. I tried to keep cool, but I confess I felt that my work was done. I knew the character of the Colonel, and also knew, that he possessed much influence with the worst class of Southerners of that section.

MANACLED AND IN PRISON.

In the meantime the constable had produced a pair of iron handcuffs, and fastened them around my wrists. After the Colonel had exhausted his supply of curses and coarse abuse upon me,—for the purpose of exciting the crowd to hang me,—I quietly asked if I would be allowed to say a few words, at the same time making a Masonic sign of distress, in hope that there might be a Mason in that crowd who would have courage sufficient to sustain my request. I had no sooner made "the sign of distress," than a voice near me said, "Yes, let's hear what he has to say"; in a moment several others spoke up and said, "He ought to be allowed to speak." I was encouraged, and very quietly said : Gentlemen, I am a total stranger here, without friends ; I am your prisoner in irons. You have charged me with violating your laws; will you act the part of cowards, by allowing this man (Col. ———) to incite you to commit a murder ; or will you, like brave men, grant the only request I have to make, that is, a fair trial before your magistrates. Several persons at once spoke up in my favour, among whom was the landlord and his brave little wife.

I was then, much to the chagrin of the Colonel, led to the lock-up, and consigned to a filthy pen.   There I remained all through that dreary night, fearing to lie down on the straw in the corner, on account of the number of vermin that infested it.   In fact, I dare not stand still through fear of being bitten by the rats that kept running about the floor all night.   At length morning came, and I was taken, hand-cuffed, weary, hungry, and filled with dread, (of what appeared my impending fate), before a Justice.

A DESPERATE SITUATION.

A crowd of people had gathered to see an abolitionist have the mockery of a trial. Col. "Legree" was asked by the Justice to state his case, which he did in true slave-driving style, as if determined to force the case against me. In fact, my case seemed hopeless.   I saw no way of escape from my desperate situation.   On every side I was surrounded by men apparently thirsting for my blood, and anxious to vindicate the outraged laws of the State of Mississippi.

At length the Colonel finished his statement, which, reduced to simple facts, was, that I had called at his residence on Saturday last, and requested permission to roam over his plantation to shoot birds; that he had given me permission, and allowed his servant "Joe" to accompany me; that "Joe" had not returned, nor could he be found; that he was sure I had aided him to escape; and demanded of the Justice that I should be punished as a "negro thief" deserved. His remarks were loudly applauded by the slave-hounds that surrounded him.

The Justice turned to me, and in a stern voice said, "Have you any thing to say?"

At this moment a voice outside the room shouted, "Here's Joe! Here's Joe!" and a rush was made toward the door.

FIDELITY OF A SLAVE.

"Joe" was ushered into the court room, and fell on his knees before the Colonel, asking his forgiveness for leaving the plantation without permission. He said he wanted to see his brother "powerful bad," and had gone to the plantation on which his brother lived, about

eight miles distant, on Saturday night, expecting
to return by Sunday evening ; but having
sprained his ancle. he could not move until
Monday evening, when he started for home,
travelling nearly all night.   As soon as he
reached the Colonel's, he was told of my arrest,
and early that morning had come into Columbus
to help me.   The Justice ordered the constable
to release me at once, and expressed his regret
that I had been subjected to so much annoyance.

RELEASED.

The Colonel was completely chopfallen at the
turn affairs had taken, while I was surrounded by
several Masonic friends, who expressed their joy
at my release.   I addressed the Colonel, saying,
that as he had put me to much inconvenience
and trouble, I claimed a favour of him.   He
asked what it was.   I begged him not to punish
"Joe" for what he had done, and to allow me to
present him with a gift as a mark of gratitude for
his fidelity to me.   As these favours were asked
in the presence of the crowd, he could not very
well refuse my request.   He sulkily promised
that "Joe" should not be punished, and said
if I pleased I might make him a present.   I then
handed "Joe" twenty dollars in gold, for which
the noble fellow looked a thousand thanks.

I was thus enabled to evince my gratitude for what he had done for me, and at the same time present him with means to aid him in escaping from bondage.

Two years after this occurrence, while dining at the American Hotel, in Boston, I observed a coloured waiter eyeing me very closely ; at last he recognised me, and asked if I remembered him. It was "Joe," my saviour, the former slave of Col. "Legree." I grasped the noble fellow's hand, and congratulated him, in the presence of all in the room, upon his escape from bondage. In the evening I invited him into the parlour, and introduced him to several influential friends, to whom, I narrated the, incidents above related. He afterwards gave me some of the particulars of his escape from slavery, as follows :—

On the Sunday evening following my arrest, his brother joined him in a piece of woods not far from Col. "Legree's" plantation, where he had secreted sufficient food to last them several days.

TWO PASSENGERS BY THE UNDERGROUND R. R.

At midnight they started together, moving as rapidly as they could through fields and woods, keeping the north star in front of them. Whenever it was possible they walked in the creeks and marshy grounds, to throw the slave-hunters off their tracks. Thus, night after night, they kept on their weary way, hungry and sorefooted. On the morning of the seventeenth day of their freedom, they reached the Ohio river, nearly opposite a large town. All day they lay secreted in the bushes, at night they found a small boat, with which they crossed the river, and travelled rapidly, taking a north-east course. They finally, after enduring many hardships, reached Cleveland, Ohio, and went to the house of a friend whose name I had given "Joe." They were kindly received, and supplied with clothing and other comforts. After a week's rest they were sent to Canada, where his brother still lives. Before leaving Boston, I secured "Joe" a good situation in a mercantile house, where he remained for many years, rendering faithful service to his grateful employers.

LEAVE COLUMBUS FOR OTHER FIELDS.

On the day following my release from peril, I took the stage for Iuka, a station on the Charleston and Memphis Railroad. There I purchased a through ticket for New York, which I took pains to exhibit to the landlord of the hotel, so that in case I was pursued, (as I certainly would be, if "Joe" and his brother succeeded in escaping), he could state the fact of my having bought tickets for New York, which would probably check their pursuit.

From Iuka I went to Huntsville, Ala., where I remained four weeks actively engaged in circulating information among the slaves. My next point was Augusta, Georgia.

AT WORK IN AUGUSTA.

Finding that Augusta was favourably situated for my work, and that the slaves in that section were sharp and intelligent, I determined to make it my next field of labour. Having secured a good home with a Quaker family, I was soon actively engaged in collecting birds and insects, and in becoming acquainted with the more intelligent coloured people of that section. I deem it my duty to place upon record the fact, that among all the religious denominations in the South, none were more faithful to the principles of freedom, or to the dictates of humanity in respect to slavery, than the sect called Quakers. Wherever I have met the members of that society, whether in the North or South, they have always proved themselves friends in deed as well as

name. They could always be implicitly trusted
by the poor fugitives flying from bondage. I
know of many instances where, at great sacrifice
and risk, they have shielded the outcasts from
their pursuers—the slave-hunters and United
States marshals. Hundreds of the negroes of
Canada will bear testimony to the unfailing
fidelity of the peaceful and worthy Quakers of
Ohio and Michigan.

ELEVEN FOLLOWERS OF THE NORTH STAR.

I laboured in Augusta for two months, and
finally succeeded in equipping a party of eleven
fine, active, intelligent slaves, for the long, dangerous, and weary journey to the north. No
one not actually engaged in similar work, can
clearly appreciate the extreme delicacy of my
position. There was not a day, in fact scarcely
an hour, that I did not live in expectation of
exposure. The system of keen and constant
espionage, in practice all over the Slave States,
rendered it exceedingly necessary to exercise
the greatest prudence in approaching the slaves.
If a stranger was seen in conversation with a
slave, he became at once an object of suspicion.
I found, by experience, that a frank, open, and
apparently indifferent course, proved the wisest.
My ostensible scientific pursuits also opened a

way for me to come in contact with the very classes of both whites and blacks best suited for my purposes.

I was greatly aided in my work in Augusta, by a remarkably intelligent negro, who was coachman to a prominent citizen of that town. This man was chosen leader of the band of fugitives from Augusta, and proved the saviour of the whole party ; for they all arrived safely in Canada in less than two months from the time of their escape from bondage. Two members of this party are now living in Canada, and in good circumstances.

On the day following the exodus of these brave fellows, I quietly left the scene of my labours, and went to Charleston, S. C.

EXCITING NEWS.

On the third day after my arrival there, one of the Charleston papers contained a despatch from Augusta, which stated that several first-class negro men had disappeared from that place within a week ; and that a very general impression prevailed there that abolitionists were at work inciting the negroes to escape from their masters. I left Charleston that evening, and went to Raleigh, N. C. While at breakfast next morning, two men seated themselves near me, and entered into a conversation relative to the escape of slaves from Augusta. One of them remarked, that an Englishman who had been stopping in Augusta for several weeks was suspected, and that it was supposed he had gone with the fugitives, as he had not been seen since the slaves were missed. He said, if the abolitionist was caught, no mercy would be shown him, as it was time an example was made of the negro thieves that infested the South.

FAST TRAVELLING TO THE NORTH.

Having finished my breakfast, I went to the office of the hotel, settled my bill, and to avoid suspicion enquired for the residence of a prominent pro-slavery man, a member of Congress. Having obtained the information, I bid the landlord good day, and left Raleigh by the first train, taking no rest until I reached Washington —nearly six months from the time I landed in New Orleans.

IN WASHINGTON.

During my stay in Washington, I became acquainted with Mr. Sumner, at whose house I had the pleasure of meeting many distinguished people, who evinced a warm and kindly interest in my labours. The slaveholders, at that period, held the balance of power in the United States, and the Democratic party was used by them to strengthen the bonds that bound the coloured people of the South in the chains of slavery.

The slave-masters were not satisfied with the recognized boundaries of their institution, and sought by every device to obtain some portion of the new territories of the south-west, in which they could carry their vile institution. Northern men of the Douglas and Seymour stamp were willing to yield to the slave lords, and even sacrifice the dearest interests of their country, providing they could advance their individual claims to the Presidency. The haughty and outrageous demands of Davis, Mason, and Toombs, were abetted by the cowardly democratic politicians of the North.

Towering above these contemptible political demagogues stood Charles Sumner, the brave champion of freedom. No prospect of political advancement could tempt him from the path of duty, Nor could the brutal threats and blows of his cowardly opponents, cause him to halt in his warfare for the rights of man.

Toward the end of April, 1858, I left Washington for Philadelphia, and laid before my anti-slavery friends a report of my work. One venerable and talented Quaker lady, at whose house our re-union took place, and whose name had long keen identified with the cause of human freedom, tendered me the hearty congratulations of the organization on my safe return from the land of darkness and despair.

TWO FUGITIVES FROM HUNTSVILLE.

While in Philadelphia a telegram was received from a friend in Evansville, Indiana, informing us that two fugitives had arrived there in a dilapidated condition, their emaciated bodies bearing the marks of many a bruise. I at once went to Evansville to render them such aid as I could. They were delighted to meet me again, and recalled an interview they had with me at Huntsville, Alabama. The poor fellows were kindly cared for, and after a few days' rest continued their journey to Canada, prepared to defend their right to own themselves against whoever might dispute it. The route travelled by these fugitives from Huntsville to the Ohio river was marked with their blood. Their escape was soon discovered, and persistent efforts made to capture

them. They were followed for two days by a
a blood-hound that was placed on their tracks,
and which they succeeded in evading, by wading
in the creeks and marshes; but for forty-eight
hours the deep baying of the hound was frequently heard. They travelled by night only,
taking the north star as their guide, and by day
they rested in secluded places. Their sufferings
from hunger were very severe, which they were
often obliged to relieve by eating frogs and
other reptiles. Occasionally they succeeded in
obtaining poultry from the hen-houses of the
farmers on their route.

From Evansville I returned to Philadelphia,
and after a short stay in that city left for Boston,
via Springfield.

CHAPTER III.

MEET WITH AN OLD FRIEND.

T Springfield, Mass., the train stopped sufficiently long to enable the passengers to get supper. As I took my seat at the table I observed an elderly gentleman looking very earnestly at me. I felt sure I had seen him before somewhere; but where and when I had quite forgotten. At length he recognized me, and taking a seat near me said, in a whisper, "How is the hardware business?" The moment he spoke I remembered the voice, and recalled my old Cleveland acquaintance, Capt. John Brown, of Kansas.

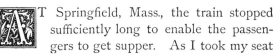

SECOND INTERVIEW WITH JOHN BROWN.

He was much changed in appearance, looking older and more careworn; his face was covered with a long beard, nearly white; his dress was plain, but good and scrupulously clean. There

John Brown

was no change in his voice or eye, both were indicative of strength, honesty, and tenacity of purpose. Learning that I was on my way to Boston, whither he was going on the following day, he urged me to remain in Springfield over night, and accompany him to Boston. After supper we retired to a private parlour, and he requested me to tell him all about my trip through Mississippi and Alabama. He remarked that our mutual friend, of Northern New York, had told him that when he last heard from me, I was in Selma. He listened to the recital of my narrative, from the time I left New Orleans until my arrest at Columbus, with intense earnestness, without speaking, until I described my arrest and imprisonment, then his countenance changed, his eyes flashed, he paced the room in fiery wrath. I never witnessed a more intense manifestation of indignation, and scorn. Coming up to me, he took my wrists in his hands and said, "God alone brought you out of that hell; and these wrists have been ironed, and you have been cast in prison for doing your duty. I vow, henceforth, that I will not rest in my labour until I have discharged my whole duty toward God, and toward my brother in bondage." When he ceased speaking he sat down and buried his face in his hands, in which position he sat for several minutes, as if overcome

4

by his feelings. At length, arousing himself, he asked me to continue my narrative, to which he listened earnestly during its recital. He said, "The Lord has permitted you to do a work that falls to the lot of but few"; taking a small Bible or Testament from his pocket, he said, "The good book says, 'Whatsoever ye would that men should do to you, do ye even so to them'; it teaches us further, to 'remember them in bonds, as bound with them.'" He continued, "I have devoted the last twenty years of my life to preparation for the work which, I believe, God has given me to do." He then gave me some details of a campaign which he was then actually preparing for, and which he said had occupied his mind for years. He intended to establish himself in the mountains of Virginia with a small body of picked men —men in whom he could trust, and who feared God. He felt confident that the negroes would flock to him in large numbers, and that the slaveholders would soon be glad to let the oppressed go free; that the dread of a negro insurrection would produce fear and trembling in all the Slave States; that the presence in the mountains of an armed body of Liberators would produce a general insurrection among the slaves, which would end in their freedom. He said he had about twenty-two Kansas men undergoing a

course of military instruction; these men would
form a nucleous, around which he would soon
gather a force sufficiently large and effective to
strike terror throughout the Slave States. His
present difficulty was, a deficiency of ready
money; he had been promised support—to help
the cause of freedom—which was not forth-
coming, now that he was preparing to carry
the war into the South. His friends were disin-
clined to aid offensive operations.

During this interview, he informed me that he
intended to call a Convention of the friends of
the cause at Chatham, Canada, in a few weeks,
for the purpose of effecting an organization
composed of men who were willing to aid him
in his purpose of invading the Slave States.
He said he had rifles and ammunition sufficient
to equip two hundred men; that he had made a
contract for a large number of pikes, with which
he intended to arm the negroes; that the
object of his present trip to the East was, to
raise funds to keep this contract, and perfect his
arrangements for an attack upon the Slave
States in the following September or October.

Captain Brown accompanied me, on the following day, to Boston. During our journey,
he informed me that he required a thousand

dollars at least to complete his preparations;
that he needed money at once to enable
him to keep a contract for arms with some
manufacturer in Connecticut. He also needed
money to bring his men from Iowa to
Canada. On our arrival in Boston, I went to
the house of a friend, and Capt. Brown took
quarters at a hotel. I saw him every day while
he remained in Boston ; and regretted to learn
that he met with but little success in obtaining
money. It appeared that those friends of the
cause of freedom, who had an inkling of his
project, were not disposed to advance money
for warlike purposes, except such as were for
the defence of free territory. He finally did
succeed in raising about five hundred dollars.
An impression prevailed, in the minds of many
sincere friends of freedom, that the persecution of himself and family by the pro-slavery
men of Kansas had so exasperated him that
he would engage in some enterprize which
would result in the destruction of himself
and followers. I am persuaded that these
impressions were groundless. I never heard
him express any feeling of personal resent-
ment towards the slaveholders. He at all
times, while in my company, appeared to be
controlled by a fixed, earnest, and unalterable
determination to do what he considered to be

his duty, as an agent in the hands of the Almighty, to give freedom to the slaves. That idea, and that alone, appeared to me to control his thoughts and actions.

On the morning of his departure from Boston, I accompanied him to the depôt, and bid him farewell. (I never again saw the brave old captain in life.) A few days afterwards, however, I received the following

LETTER FROM CAPT. BROWN.

CHATHAM, CANADA,
May 5th, 1858.

MY DEAR FRIEND,
I have called a *quiet* Convention in this place of *true* friends of freedom. Your attendance is earnestly requested on the 10th inst.   *   *   *   *

Your Friend,
(*Fac-simile of Signature.*)

John Brown

In consequence of my absence from Boston, I did not receive the above letter until the 13th of May—three days after the time appointed for the meeting of the Convention.

REFUGEES IN CANADA.

During the summer of 1858 I visited Canada, and had great pleasure in meeting several of those who had, under my auspices, escaped from the land of bondage.   In a barber shop, in Hamilton, I was welcomed by a man who had escaped from Augusta, and who kept, as a *souvenir* of my friendship, a dirk knife I had given him on the night he started for Canada. The meeting with so many of my former pupils, and the fact that they were happy, thriving, and industrious, gave me great satisfaction.   The trials and dangers I had endured in their behalf were pleasing reminiscences to me, when surrounded by the prosperous and happy people whom I had striven to benefit.

The information I obtained from the Canadian refugees, relative to their experiences while *en route* to Canada, enabled me in after years to render most valuable aid to other fugitives from the land of bondage.

On the 9th of October, 1859, I was surprised to receive the following letter from Captain Brown, announcing his determination to make an attack on the slave States in the course of a few weeks. The letter reads as follows :—

CHAMBERSBURG, PENN.,
October 6th, 1859.

DEAR FRIEND,

I shall *move* about the last of this month.
Can you help *the cause* in the way promised?
Address your reply to Isaac Smith, Chambers-
burg, Penn. *   *   *   *   *   *

Your friend,

JOHN BROWN.

IN RICHMOND.

Soon after the reception of the above letter I
left for Richmond, Virginia, much against the
wishes of my friends. I had promised Captain
Brown, during our interview at Springfield, Mass.,
that when he was ready to make his attack on
the Slave States, I would go to Richmond and
await the result.   In case he should be successful in his attack, I would be in a position to
watch the course of events, and enlighten the
slaves as to his purposes.   It might also be possible for me to aid the cause in other respects.
On my arrival in Richmond, I went to the house
of an old friend, with whom I had stopped during
my previous raid on the chattels of Virginia's
slaveholders.

CAPTAIN BROWN ATTACKS HARPER'S FERRY.

On the morning of Monday, the 17th of
October, wild rumours were in circulation about
the streets of Richmond that Harper's Ferry had
been captured by a band of robbers; and, again,
that an army of abolitionists, under the command
of a desperado by the name of Smith, was murdering the inhabitants of that village, and carrying off the negroes. Throughout the day, groups
of excited men gathered about the newspaper
offices to hear the news from Harper's Ferry.

On the following morning (Tuesday) an official
report was received, which stated the fact that a
small force of abolitionists, under old Ossawatomie
Brown, had taken possession of the U. S. building at the Ferry, and had entrenched themselves.
I met an aged negro in the street, who seemed
completely bewildered about the excitement and
military preparations going on around him. As
I approached him, he lifted his hat and said:
"Please massa, what's the matter? What's the
soldiers called out for?" I told him a band
of abolitionists had seized Harper's Ferry, and
liberated many of the slaves of that section;
that they intended to free all the slaves in the
South, if they could. "Can dey do it, massa?"
he asked, while his countenance brightened up.

I replied by asking him, if he wished to be free? He said: "O yes, massa; I'se prayed for dat dese forty years. My two boys are way off in Canada. Do you know whar dat is, massa?" I told him I was a Canadian, which seemed to give him a great surprise. He said his two boys had run away from their master, because he threatened to take them to New Orleans for sale.

That John Brown had struck a blow that resounded throughout the Slave States was evident, from the number of telegraph despatches from all the Slave States, offering aid to crush the invasion.

DEFEAT OF CAPTAIN BROWN.

The people of Richmond were frantic with rage at this daring interference with their cherished institution, which gave them the right to buy, beat, work, and sell their fellow men. Crowds of rough, excited men, filled with whiskey and wickedness, stood for hours together in front of the offices of the *Despatch* and *Enquirer*, listening to the reports as they were announced from within. When the news of Brown's defeat and capture, and the destruction of his little army, was read from the window of the *Despatch* office, the vast crowds set up a demoniac yell of delight, which to me sounded like a death knell to all my hopes for the freedom of the enslaved. As the excitement was hourly increasing, and threats made to search the city for abolitionists, I saw that nothing could be gained by remaining in Richmond. I left for Washington, nearly crushed in spirit at the destruction of Captain Brown and his noble little band. On the train were Southerners from many of the Slave States, who expressed their views of Northern abolitionists in the most emphatic slave-driving language. The excitement was intense, every stranger, especially if he looked like a Northerner, was closely watched, and in some instances subjected to inquisition.

DOUGH-FACED NORTHERNERS.

The attitude of many of the leading Northern politicians and so-called statesmen, in Washington, was actually disgusting. These weak-kneed and craven creatures were profuse in their apologies for Brown's assault, and hastened to divest themselves of what little manhood they possessed, when in the presence of the braggarts and women-whippers of the South. "What can we do to conciliate the Slave States?" was the leading question of the day. Such men as Crittenden, and Douglas, were ready to compromise with the slaveholders even at the sacrifice of their avowed principles. While Toombs, Davis, Mason, Slidell, and the rest of the slave-driving crew, haughtily demanded further guarantees for the protection of their "institution;" and had it not been for the stand taken by the people of the Northern States at that time, their political leaders would have bound the North, hand and foot, to do the bidding of the slaveholders. But on that occasion, as well as all others where the principles of freedom have been involved, the people of the United States were found worthy descendants of their revolutionary sires.

EFFECTS OF JOHN BROWN'S ATTACK.

The blow struck at Harper's Ferry, which the Democratic leaders affected to ridicule, had startled the slaveholders from their dreams of security, and sent fear and trembling into every home in the Slave States. On every plantation the echoes from Harper's Ferry were heard. The poor terrified slave, as he laid down at night, weary from his enforced labours, offered up a prayer to God for the safety of the grand old captain, who was a prisoner in the hands of merciless enemies, who were thirsting for his blood.

BRAVERY OF CAPTAIN BROWN.

How bravely John Brown bore himself while in the presence of the human wolves that surrounded him, as he lay mangled and torn in front of the engine-house at Harper's Ferry! Mason, of Virginia, and that Northern renegade, Vallandigham, interrogated the apparently dying man, trying artfully, but in vain, to get him to implicate leading Northern men. In the history of modern times there is not recorded another instance of such rare heroic valour as John Brown displayed in the presence of Governor Wise, of Virginia. How contemptible are Mason, Wise, and Vallandigham, when compared with the wounded old soldier, as he lay weltering in his blood, and near him his two sons, Oliver and Watson, cold in death. Mason and Vallandigham died with the stain of treason on their heads, while Governor Wise, who signed Brown's death warrant, still lives, despised and abhorred.

To superficial observers, Brown's attack on Virginia with so small a force, looked like the act of a madman ; but those who knew John Brown, and the men under his command, are satisfied that if he had carried out his original plans, and retreated with his force to the mountains, after he had captured the arms in the arsenal, he could have defeated and baffled any force sent against him. The slaves would have flocked to his standard in thousands, and the slaveholders would have trembled with fear for the safety of their families.

JOHN BROWN VICTORIOUS.

John Brown in prison, surrounded by his captors, won greater victories than if he had conquered the South by force of arms. His courage, truthfulness, humanity, and self-sacrificing devotion to the cause of the poor downtrodden slaves, shamed the cowardly, weak-kneed, and truculent Northern politicians into opposition to the haughty demands of the despots of the South.

"HIS SOUL IS MARCHING ON."

Virginia, in her pride and strength, judicially murdered John Brown. But the day is not far distant when the freedmen and freemen of the South will erect a monument on the spot where his gallows once stood, to perpetuate to all coming generations the noble self-sacrifice of that brave Christian martyr. And when the Southern statesmen who shouted for his execution are mouldering in the silent dust, forgotten or unpleasantly remembered, the memory of John Brown will grow brighter and brighter through all coming ages.

JOHN BROWN'S MARTYRDOM.

December the 2nd, was the day appointed for the execution of Capt. Brown. I determined to make an effort to see him once more if possible. Taking the cars at Baltimore, on Nov. 26th, I went to Harper's Ferry and applied to the military officer in command for permission to go to Charleston. He enquired what object I had in view in wishing to go there at that time, while so much excitement existed. I replied, that I had a desire to see John Brown once more before his death. Without replying to me, he called an officer in the room and directed him to place me in close confinement until the train for Baltimore came, and then to place me on board, and command the conductor to take me to Baltimore. Then, raising his voice, he said, "Captain, if he (myself) returns to Harper's Ferry, shoot him at once." I was placed under guard until the train came in, when, in despite of my protests, I was taken to Baltimore. Determined to make one more attempt, I went to Richmond to try and obtain a pass from the Governor. After much difficulty I obtained an

INTERVIEW WITH GOVERNOR WISE.

I told the Governor that I had a strong desire to see John Brown before his execution ; that I had some acquaintance with him, and had formed a very high estimate of him as a man. I asked him to allow me to go to Charlestown (under *surveillance* if he pleased), and bid the old Captain "Good bye." The Governor made many inquiries as to my relation to Brown, and whether I justified his attack on Virginia. I replied candidly, stating that I had from childhood been an ardent admirer of Washington, Jefferson, and Madison, and that all these great and good men deplored the existence of slavery in the Republic. That my admiration and friendship for John Brown was owing to his holding similar views, and his earnest desire to abolish the evil. The Governor looked at me with amazement, and for a moment made no reply. At length he straightened himself up, and, assuming a dignified look, said, "My family motto is, '*sapere aude.*' I am *wise* enough to understand your object in wishing to go to Charlestown, and I *dare* you to go. If you attempt it, I will have you shot. It is just such men as you who have urged Brown to make his crazy attack on our constitutional rights and privileges. You shall not leave Richmond until after the execution of Brown. I wish I could hang a dozen of your leading abolitionists."

HE WOULD LIKE TO BAG GIDDINGS AND GERRIT SMITH.

"If I could *bag* old Giddings and Gerrit Smith, I would hang them without trial." The Governor was now greatly excited, and, rising from his chair, he said, "No, sir! you shall not leave Richmond. You shall go to prison, and remain there until next Monday; then you may go North, and slander the State which ought to have hanged you." I quietly waited a moment before replying, and then remarked, that as he refused me permission to see Capt. Brown, I would leave Virginia at once, and thus save both him and the State any trouble or expense on my account. I said this very quietly, while his keen eyes were riveted on me. In reply, he said, "Did I not tell you that you should remain a prisoner here until Monday?" I quietly said, "Yes, Governor, you certainly did; but I am sure the executive of this great State is too *wise* to fear one unarmed man." For a few moments he tapped the table with his fingers, without saying anything. Then he came toward me, shaking his fore finger, and said: "Well, you may go; and I would advise you to tell your Giddings, Greeleys, and Garrisons, cowards that they are, to lead the next raid on Virginia themselves."

Fearing that obstacles might be thrown in my way which would cause detention and trouble, I requested the Governor to give me a permit to leave the State of Virginia. Without making any reply, he picked up a blank card, and wrote as follows :—

"The bearer, is hereby ordered to leave the State of Virginia within twenty-four hours."
(*Fac-simile of Signature.*)

Henry A. Wise

This he handed me, saying, "The sooner you go, the better for you: our people are greatly excited, and you may regret this visit, if you stay another hour."

I returned to Philadelphia as rapidly as possible, where I remained until the remains of Capt. Brown arrived, *en route* for their final resting place at North Elba, in Northern New York. Having taken my last look at the dead liberator, I returned to Canada, where I remained until my preparations were completed for another visit to the South.

5

EXTRACTS FROM THE PRESS OF THAT PERIOD.

The following Extracts from the Press of that period, will furnish my readers with a good index of the popular feeling respecting John Brown's raid, and his defeat, imprisonment, trial, and execution :—

From *Harper's Weekly*, October 29, 1859.

EXTRAORDINARY INSURRECTION AT HARPER'S FERRY.

One of the most extraordinary events that ever occurred in our history took place last week at Harper's Ferry. We shall endeavour to give our readers a connected history of the affair, which, at the present time, has been brought to a close.

THE FIRST ACTIVE MOVEMENT.

The first active movement in the insurrection was made at about half-past ten o'clock on Sunday night. William Williamson, the watchman at Harper's Ferry bridge, while walking across toward the Maryland side, was seized by a number of men, who said he was their

prisoner, and must come with them. He recognized Brown and Cook among the men, and
knowing them, treated the matter as a joke,
but enforcing silence, they conducted him to the
Armory, which he found already in their possession. He was detained till after daylight, and
then discharged. The watchman who was to
relieve Williamson at midnight found the bridge
lights all out, and was immediately seized.
Supposing it an attempt at robbery, he broke
away, and his pursuers stumbling over him, he
escaped.

ARREST OF COLONEL WASHINGTON AND OTHERS.

The next appearance of the insurrectionists
was at the house of Colonel Lewis Washington,
a large farmer and slave-owner, living about
four miles from the ferry. A party, headed
by Cook, proceeded there, and rousing Colonel
Washington, told him he was their prisoner.
They also seized all the slaves near the house,
took a carriage horse, and a large waggon with
two horses. When Colonel Washington saw
Cook, he immediately recognized him as the
man who had called upon him some months
previous, to whom he had exhibited some valuable arms in his possession, including an antique
sword presented by Frederick the Great to

George Washington, and a pair of pistols presented by Lafayette to Washington, both being
heir-looms in the family.   Before leaving, Cook
wanted Colonel Washington to engage in a trial
of skill at shooting, and exhibited considerable
skill as a marksman.   When he made the visit
on Sunday night he alluded to his previous
visit, and the courtesy with which he had been
treated, and regretted the necessity which made
it his duty to arrest Colonel Washington.   He,
however, took advantage of the knowledge he
had obtained by his former visit to carry off
all the valuable collection of arms, which the
Colonel did not re-obtain till after the final
defeat of the insurrection.

From Colonel Washington's he proceeded with
him as a prisoner in the carriage, and twelve of
his negroes in the waggon, to the house of Mr.
Alstadt, another large farmer, on the same road.
Mr. Alstadt and his son, a lad of sixteen, were
taken prisoners, and all their negroes within
reach forced to join the movement.   He then
returned to the Armory at the Ferry.

THE STOPPAGE OF THE RAILROAD TRAIN.

At the upper end of the town the mail train
arrived at the usual hour, when a coloured man,

who acted as assistant to the baggage-master, was shot, receiving a mortal wound, and the conductor, Mr. Phelps, was threatened with violence if he attempted to proceed with the train. Feeling uncertain as to the condition of affairs, the conductor waited until after daylight before he ventured to proceed, having delayed the train six hours.

Luther Simpson, baggage-master of the mail-train, gives the following particulars: I walked up the bridge; was stopped, but was afterward permitted to go up and see the captain of the insurrectionists; I was taken to the Armory, and saw the captain, whose name is Bill Smith; I was kept prisoner for more than an hour, and saw from five to six hundred negroes, all having arms; there were two or three hundred white men with them; all the houses were closed. I went into a tavern kept by Mr. Chambers; thirty of the inhabitants were collected there with arms. They said most of the inhabitants had left, but they declined, preferring to protect themselves; it was reported that five or six persons had been shot.

Mr. Simpson was escorted back over the bridge by six negroes.

THE STATE OF AFFAIRS AT DAYBREAK.

It was not until the town thoroughly waked up, and found the bridge guarded by armed men, and a guard stationed at all the avenues, that the people saw that they were prisoners. A panic appears to have immediately ensued, and the number of insurrectionists was at once largely increased. In the mean time a number of workmen, not knowing anything of what had occurred, entered the Armory, and were successively taken prisoners, until at one time they had not less than sixty men confined in the Armory. These were imprisoned in the engine-house, which afterward became the chief fortress of the insurgents, and were not released until after the final assault. The workmen were imprisoned in a large building further down the yard.

EARLY CASUALTIES.

A coloured man, named Hayward, a railroad porter, was shot early in the morning for refusing to join in the movement.

The next man shot was Joseph Burley, a citizen of Perry. He was shot standing in his own door. The insurrectionists by this time, finding a disposition to resist them, had withdrawn nearly all within the Armory grounds, leaving only a guard on the bridge.

About this time, also, Samuel P. Young, Esq., was shot dead. He was coming into town on horseback, carrying a gun, when he was shot from the Armory, receiving a wound of which he died during the day. He was a graduate of West Point, and greatly respected in the neighbourhood for his high character and noble qualities.

The lawn in front of the engine-house after the assault presented a dreadful sight. Lying on it were two bodies of men killed on the previous day, and found inside the house ; three wounded men, one of them just at the last gasp of life, and two others groaning in pain. One of the dead was Brown's son. Oliver, the wounded man, and his son Watson, were lying on the grass, the father presenting a gory spectacle. He had a severe bayonet wound in his side, and his face and hair were clotted with blood.

APPEARANCE OF THE PRISONERS.

When the insurgents were brought out, some dead, others wounded, they were greeted with execrations, and only the precautions that had been taken saved them from immediate execution. The crowd, nearly every man of which carried a gun, swayed with tumultuous excitement, and cries of "Shoot them! shoot them!" rang from every side. The appearance of the liberated prisoners, all of whom, through the steadiness of the marines, escaped injury, changed the current of feeling, and prolonged cheers took the place of howls and execrations.

BROWN'S EXAMINATION.

A short time after Captain Brown was brought out, he revived and talked earnestly to those about him, defending his course, and avowing that he had done only what was right. He replied to questions substantially as follows : "Are you Captain Brown, of Kansas?" "I am sometimes called so." "Are you Ossawatamie Brown?" "I tried to do my duty there." "What was your present object ?" " To free the slaves from bondage." "Were any other persons but those with you now connected with the movement ?" "No." "Did you expect aid from the North?" "No ; there was no one connected with the movement but those who came with me." "Did you expect to kill people to carry your point ?" "I did not wish to do so, but you force us to it." Various questions of this kind were put to

Captain Brown, which he answered clearly and freely, with seeming anxiety to vindicate himself. He urged that he had the town at his mercy : that he could have burned it, and murdered the inhabitants, but did not ; he had treated the prisoners with courtesy, and complained that he was hunted down like a beast. He spoke of the killing of his son, which he alleged was done while bearing a flag of truce, and seemed very anxious for the safety of his wounded son. His conversation bore the impression of the conviction that whatever he had done to free the slaves was right ; and that, in the warfare in which he was engaged, he was entitled to be treated with all the respect of a prisoner of war.

CAPTURE OF ARMS.

During Tuesday morning, one of Washington's negroes came in and reported that Captain Cook was on the mountain, only three miles off ; about the same time some shots were said to have been fired from the Maryland hills, and a rapid fusilade was returned from Harper's Ferry. The Independent Grays of Baltimore immediately started on a scouting expedition, and in two hours returned with two waggons loaded with arms and ammunition, found at Captain Brown's house.

The arms consisted of boxes filled with Sharp's rifles, pistols, &c., all bearing the stamp of the Massachusetts Manufacturing Company, Chicopee, Mass. There were also found a quantity of United States ammunition, a large number of spears, sharp iron bowie-knives fixed upon poles, a terrible looking weapon, intended for the use of the negroes, with spades, pickaxes, shovels, and everything else that might be needed : thus proving that the expedition was well provided for, that a large party of men were expected to be armed, and that abundant means had been provided to pay all expenses.

How all these supplies were got up to this farm without attracting observation, is very strange. They are supposed to have been brought through Pennsylvania. The Grays pursued Cook so fast that they secured a part of his arms, but with his more perfect knowledge of localities, he was enabled to evade them.

TREATMENT OF BROWN'S PRISONERS.

The citizens imprisoned by the insurrectionists all testify to their lenient treatment. They were neither tied nor insulted, and, beyond the outrage of restricting their liberty, were not ill-used. Capt. Brown was always courteous to them, and at all times assured them that they would not be injured. He explained his purposes to them, and while he had them (the workmen) in confinement, made no abolition speech to them. Colonel Washington speaks of him as a man of extraordinary nerve. He never blanched during the assault, though he admitted in the night that escape was impossible, and that he would have to die. When the door was broken down, one of his men exclaimed, " I surrender." The Captain immediately cried out, " There's one surrenders ; give him quarter ;" and at the same moment fired his own rifle at the door.

During the previous night he spoke freely with Colonel Washington, and referred to his sons. He said he had lost one in Kansas and two here. He had not pressed them to join him in the expedition, but did not regret their loss—they had died in a glorious cause.

BROWN'S PAPERS AND STORES.

On the 18th a detachment of marines and some volunteers made a visit to Brown's house. They found a large quantity of blankets, boots, shoes, clothes, tents, and fifteen hundred pikes, with large blades affixed. They also discovered

a carpet-bag, containing documents throwing
much light on the affair, printed constitutions
and by-laws of an organization, showing or indicating ramifications in various States of the
Union.   They also found letters from various individuals at the North—one from Fred. Douglass,
containing ten dollars from a lady for the cause ;
also a letter from Gerrit Smith about money
matters, and a check or draft by him for $100,
indorsed by the cashier of a New York bank,
name not recollected.   All these are in possession of Governor Wise.

HIS WARNING TO THE SOUTH.

Reporter of the *Herald.*—I do not wish to
annoy you ; but, if you have any thing further
you would like to say, I will report it.

Mr. Brown.—I have nothing to say, only that
I claim to be here in carrying out a measure I
believe perfectly justifiable, and not to act the
part of an incendiary or ruffian, but to aid those
suffering great wrong.   I wish to say, furthermore, that you had better—all you people at
the South—prepare yourselves for a settlement
of that question that must come up for settlement sooner than you are prepared for it.   The
sooner you are prepared the better.   You may

dispose of me very easily. I am nearly disposed of now ; but this question is still to be settled— this negro question, I mean ; the end of that is not yet. These wounds were inflicted upon me —both sabre cuts on my head and bayonet stabs on different parts of my body—some minutes after I had ceased fighting, and had consented to a surrender, for the benefit of others, not for my own. (This statement was vehemently denied by all around.) I believe the Major (meaning Lieutenant J. B. Stuart, of the United States Cavalry) would not have been alive—I could have killed him just as easy as a mosquito when he came in, but I supposed he came in only to receive our surrender. There had been loud and long calls of "surrender" from us—as loud as men could yell—but in the confusion and excitement I suppose we were not heard. I do not think the Major, or any one, meant to butcher us after we had surrendered.

BROWN'S VIEWS.

Brown has had a conversation with Senator Mason, which is reported in the *Heerald*. The following is a *verbatim* report of the conversation :—

Mr. Mason.—Can you tell us, at least, who furnished money for your expedition ?

Mr. Brown.—I furnished most of it myself. I can not implicate others. It is by my own folly' that I have been taken. I could easily have saved myself from it had I exercised my own better judgment, rather than yielded to my feelings.

Mr. Mason.—You mean if you had escaped immediately?

Mr. Brown.—No; I had the means to make myself secure without any escape, but I allowed myself to be surrounded by a force by being too tardy.

*   *   *   *   *   *

Mr. Mason.—But you killed some people passing along the streets quietly.

Mr. Brown.—Well, sir, if there was any thing of that kind done it was without my knowledge. Your own citizens, who were my prisoners, will tell you that every possible means was taken to prevent it. I did not allow my men to fire, nor even to return a fire, when there was danger of killing those we regarded as innocent persons, if I could help it. They will tell you that we allowed ourselves to be fired at repeatedly, and did not return it.

A By-stander.—That is not so. You killed an unarmed man at the corner of the house over there (at the water tank), and another besides.

Mr. Brown.—See here, my friend, it is useless to dispute or contradict the report of your own neighbors who were my prisoners.

Mr. Mason.—If you would tell us who sent you here—who provided the means—that would be information of some value.

Mr. Brown.—I will answer freely and faithfully about what concerns myself—I will answer any thing I can with honor, but not about others.

* * * * * *

Mr. Mason.—How many are engaged with you in this movement? I ask those questions for our own safety.

Mr. Brown.—Any questions that I can honorably answer I will, not otherwise. So far as I am myself concerned, I have told every thing truthfully. I value my word, sir.

Mr. Mason.—What was your object in coming?

Mr. Brown.—We came to free the slaves, and only that.)

A Young Man (in the uniform of a volunteer company).—How many men in all had you?

Mr. Brown.—I came to Virginia with eighteen men only, besides myself.

Volunteer.—What in the world did you suppose you could do here in Virginia with that amount of men?

Mr. Brown.—Young man, I don't wish to discuss that question here.

Volunteer.—You could not do any thing.

Mr. Brown.—Well, perhaps your ideas and mine on military subjects would differ materially.

Mr. Mason.—How do you justify your acts?

Mr. Brown.—I think, my friend, you are guilty of a great wrong against God and humanity—I say it without wishing to be offensive—and it would be perfectly right for any one to interfere with you so far as to free those you wilfully and wickedly hold in bondage. I do not say this insultingly.

Mr. Mason.—I understand that.

Mr. Brown.—I think I did right, and that others will do right who interfere with you at any time and all times. I hold that the golden rule, " Do unto others as you would that others should do unto you," applies to all who would help others to gain their liberty.

HOW HE WAS COMMANDER-IN-CHIEF.

*   *   *   *   *   *

Mr. Mason.—Did you consider this a military organization, in this paper (the Constitution)? I have not read it.

Mr. Brown.—I did in some sense. ·I wish you would give that paper close attention.

Mr. Mason.—You considered yourself the Commander-in-Chief of these " provisional " military forces?

Mr. Brown.—I was chosen, agreeably to the ordinance of a certain document, Commander-in-Chief of that force.

Mr. Mason.—What wages did you offer?

Mr. Brown.—None.

Lieutenant Stuart.—" The wages of sin is death."

Mr. Brown.—I would not have made such a

6

remark to you if you had been a prisoner and wounded in my hands.

A By-stander.—Did you not promise a negro in Gettysburg twenty dollars a month?

Mr. Brown.—I did not.

By-stander.—He says you did.

WHAT HE EXPECTED.

*   *   *   *   *   *

Mr. Vallandigham.—Did you expect a general rising of the slaves in case of your success?

Mr. Brown.—No, sir; nor did I wish it. I expected to gather them up from time to time and set them free.

Mr. Vallandigham.—Did you expect to hold possession here till then?

Mr. Brown.—Well, probably I had quite a different idea. I do not know that I ought to reveal my plans. I am here a prisoner and wounded, because I foolishly allowed myself to be so. You overrate your strength in supposing I could have been taken if I had not allowed it. I was too tardy after commencing the open attack—in delaying my movements through Monday night, and up to the time I was attacked by the Government troops.) It was all occasioned by my desire to spare the feelings of my prisoners and their families and the community at large. I had no knowledge of the shooting of the negro (Heywood).

Mr. Vallandigham.—What time did you commence your organization in Canada.

Mr. Brown.—That occurred about two years ago, if I remember right. It was, I think, in 1858.

Mr. Vallandigham.—Who was the secretary?

Mr. Brown.—That I could not tell if I recollected, but I do not recollect. I think the officers were elected in May, 1858. I may answer incorrectly, but not intentionally. My head is a little confused by wounds, and my memory obscure on dates, etc.

PERSONAL APPEARANCE OF THE INSURGENTS.

A writer in the Baltimore *Exchange*, gives the following account of the personal appearance of the insurgents :—

Old Brown, the leader, is a small man, with white head, and cold-looking grey eyes. When not speaking his lips are compressed, and he has the appearance of a most determined man. His two sons (one dead) were strikingly alike in their personal appearance. Each about five feet eleven inches high, with spare visage, sallow complexion, sunken eyes, and dark hair and beard. The beard was sparse and long, and their hair long and matted. The wounded man is of undoubted courage, and from his cold sullen manner, one would suppose did not ask for or desire sympathy. Anderson, mortally wounded, is tall, black-haired, and of dark complexion. His appearance is indicative of desperate resolution. Although suffering the most intense agony from the wound in the abdomen, he did not complain, or ask for any favour, and the only evidence he gave of suffering, was occasionally a slight groan. He looks to be thirty years of age. Stevens, who was wounded on Monday afternoon, and taken prisoner, is physically a model man. He is five feet eleven inches high, with fine brawny shoulders and large sinewy limbs, all the muscles finely developed and hard. He is of dark complexion, and of undoubted resolution. When taken prisoner, he did not ask or expect quarter, and lay and suffered from his wounds without complaint other than a groan.

COMMENCEMENT OF THE TRIAL.

A fresh attempt of Brown's to have the trial postponed in order to obtain counsel from the

North having failed, the case was proceeded with.

The jury having been sworn to fairly and impartially try the prisoner, the Court directed that the prisoner might forego the form of standing while arraigned, if he desired it.

Mr. Botts put the enquiry to the prisoner, and he continued to lie prostrate on his cot while the long indictment, filling seven pages, was read :

First—For conspiring with negroes to produce insurrection ;

Second—For treason to the Commonwealth ; and,

Third—For murder.

THE SPEECHES AND THE EVIDENCE.

The case was then opened at length by Messrs. Harding and Hunter for the Commonwealth, and by Messrs. Botts and Green for the prisoner.

OLD BROWN ASKS FOR DELAY.

Mr. Brown then arose, and said : " I do not intend to detain the Court, but barely wish to say, as I have been promised a fair trial, that I am not now in circumstances that enable me to attend a trial, owing to the state of my health. I have a severe wound in the back, or rather in one kidney, which enfeebles me very much. But I am doing well; and I only ask for a very short delay of my trial, and I think that I may be able to listen to it; and I merely ask this, that as the saying is, 'the devil may have his dues'—no more. I wish to say further, that my hearing is impaired and rendered indistinct in consequence of wounds I have about my head. I cannot hear distinctly at all; I could not hear what the Court has said this morning. I would be glad to hear what is said on my trial, and am now doing better than I could expect to be under the circumstances. A very short delay would be all I would ask. I do not presume to ask more than a very short delay, so that I may in some degree recover, and be able at least to listen to my trial, and hear what questions are asked of the citizens, and what their answers are. If that could be allowed me, I should be very much obliged.

At the conclusion of Brown's remarks, the Court assigned Charles J. Faulkner and Lawson Botts as counsel for the prisoners.

THE EXAMINATION BEFORE THE MAGISTRATE.

The examination before the magistrates then proceeded. The evidence given was much the same as that which we published last week. It established the main facts charged against Brown, but showed that he had treated the prisoners humanely. At the close of the examination, the case was given to the Grand Jury, who found a true bill next day.

THE ARRAIGNMENT.

At twelve o'clock on the 26th, the Court reassembled. The Grand Jury reported a true bill against the prisoners, and were discharged.

Charles B. Harding, assisted by Andrew Hunter, represented the Commonwealth ; and Charles J. Faulkner and Lawson Botts are counsel for the prisoners.

A true bill was read against each prisoner:

First—For conspiring with negroes to produce insurrection ;

Second—For treason to the Commonwealth ; and,

Third—For murder.

The prisoners were brought into Court accompanied by a body of armed men. They passed through the streets and entered the Court-house without the slightest demonstration on the part of the people.

Brown looked somewhat better, and his eye was not so much swollen. Stevens had to be supported, and reclined on a mattress on the floor of the Court-room, evidently unable to sit. He has the appearance of a dying man, breathing with great difficulty.

Before the reading of the arraignment, Mr. Hunter called the attention of the Court to the necessity of appointing additional counsel for the prisoners, stating that one of the counsel (Faulkner) appointed by the County Court, considering his duty in that capacity as having ended, had left. The prisoners, therefore, had no other counsel than Mr. Botts. If the Court was about to assign them other counsel, it might be proper to do so now.

The Court stated that it would assign them any member of the bar they might select.

After consulting Captain Brown, Mr. Botts said that the prisoner retained him, and desired to have Mr. Green, his assistant, to assist him. If the Court would accede to that arrangement it would be very agreeable to him personally.

The Court requested Mr. Green to act as counsel for the prisoner, and he consented to do so.

Old Brown addressed the Court as follows :—

Virginians.—I did not ask for any quarter at the time I was taken. I did not ask to have my life spared. The Governor of the State of Virginia tendered me his assurance that I should have a fair trial ; but under no circumstances whatever will I be able to have a fair trial. If you seek my blood, you can have it at any moment, without this mockery of a trial. I have had no counsel ; I have not been able to advise with any one. I know nothing about the feelings of my fellow prisoners, and am utterly unable to attend in any way to my own defence. My memory don't serve me ; my health is insufficient, although improving. There are mitigating circumstances that I would urge in our favour if a fair trial is to be allowed us ; but if we are to be farced with a mere form— a trial for execution—you might spare your selves that trouble. I am ready for my fate.

I do not ask a trial. I beg for no mockery of a trial—no insult—nothing but that which conscience gives or cowardice would drive you to practise. I ask again to be excused from the mockery of a trial. I do not even know what the special design of this examination is. I do not know what is to be the benefit of it to the Commonwealth. I have now little further to ask, other than that I may not be foolishly insulted, only as cowardly barbarians insult those who fall into their power.

THE TRIAL OF JOHN BROWN.

On Monday, 31st ult., Mr. Griswold summed up for the defence, and Mr. Harding for the Commonwealth of Virginia.

During most of the arguments Brown lay on his back, with his eyes closed.

Mr. Chilton asked the Court to instruct the jury, if they believe the prisoner was not a citizen of Virginia, but of another State, they cannot convict on a count of treason.

The Court declined, saying the Constitution did not give rights and immunities alone, but also imposed responsibilities.

Mr. Chilton asked another instruction, to the effect that the jury must be satisfied that the place where the offence was committed was within the boundaries of Jefferson County, which the Court granted.

A recess was taken up for half an hour, when the jury came in with a verdict.

There was intense excitement.

Brown sat up in bed while the verdict was rendered.

The jury found him guilty of treason, advising and conspiring with slaves and others to rebel, and for murder in the first degree.

Brown lay down quickly, and said nothing.

There was no demonstration of any kind.

MOTION IN ARREST OF JUDGMENT.

Mr. Chilton moved an arrest of judgment, both on account of errors in the indictment and errors in the verdict. The prisoner had been tried for an offence not appearing on the record of the Grand Jury ; the verdict was not on each count separately, but was a general verdict on the whole indictment.

On the following day Mr. Griswold stated the
point on which an arrest of judgment was asked
for in Brown's case. He said it had not been
proved beyond a doubt that he (Brown) was
even a citizen of the United States, and argued
that treason could not be committed against a
State, but only against the General Government,
citing the authority of Judge Story ; also stating
the jury had not found the prisoner guilty of the
crimes as charged in the indictment—they had
not responded to the offences, but found him
guilty of offences not charged. They find him
guilty of murder in the first degree, when the
indictment don't charge him with offences con-
stituting that crime.

Mr. Hunter replied, quoting the Virginia code
to the effect that technicalities should not arrest
the administration of justice. As to the jurisdiction over treason, it was sufficient to say that
Virginia had passed a law assuming that jurisdiction, and defining what constituted that
crime.

On the following day the Court gave its
decision as ruling the objections made. In the
objection that treason cannot be committed
against a State, he ruled that wherever alle-
giance is due, treason may be committed. Most

of the States have passed laws against treason. The objections as to the form of the verdict rendered, the Court also regarded as insufficient.

The clerk then asked Mr. Brown whether he had anything to say why sentence should not be passed upon him.

Mr. Brown immediately rose, and, in a clear, distinct voice, said: "I have, may it please the Court, a few words to say. I deny every thing but what I have all along admitted, of a design on my part to free slaves. I intended, certainly, to have made a clean thing of that matter, as I did last winter, when I went into Missouri, and there took slaves without the snapping of a gun on either side, moving them through the country, and finally leaving them in Canada. I designed to have done the same thing again on a larger scale. That was all I intended. I never did intend murder or treason, or the destruction of property, or to excite or incite slaves to rebellion, or to make insurrection.) I have another objection, and that is, that it is unjust that I should suffer such a penalty. Had I interfered in the manner in which I admit, and which I admit had been fairly proved—for I admire the truthfulness and candor of the greater portion of the witnesses who have testified in this case—had I so interfered in behalf of the rich, the powerful, the intelligent, the so-called great, or in behalf of any of their friends, either father, mother, brother, sister, wife, or children, or any of that class, and suffered and sacrificed what I have in this interference, it would have been all right ; every man in this Court would have deemed it an act worthy of reward rather than punishment.

AN APPEAL TO THE BIBLE.

"This Court acknowledges, too, as I suppose, the validity of the law of God. I see a book kissed, which I suppose to be the Bible, or at least the New Testament, which teaches me that all things whatsoever I would that men should do to me, I should do even so to them. It teaches me, further, to remember them that are in bonds as bound with them. I endeavoured to act up to that instruction. I say I am yet too young to understand that God is any respecter of persons. I believe that to have interfered as I have done, as I have always freely admitted I have done, in behalf of His despised poor, is no wrong, but right. Now, if it is deemed necessary that I should forfeit my life for the furtherance of the ends of justice, and mingle my blood further with the blood of my children and with the blood of millions in this slave country, whose

rights are disregarded by wicked, cruel, and unjust enactments, I say let be done, Let me say
one word further. I feel entirely satisfied with
the treatment I have received on my trial. Considering all the circumstances, it has been more
generous than I expected ; but I feel no con-
sciousness of guilt. I have stated from the first
what was my intention, and what was not. I
never had any design against the liberty of any
person, nor any disposition to commit treason or
incite slaves to rebel or make any general insurrection. I never encouraged any man to do so,
but always discouraged any idea of that kind.
Let me say, also, in regard to the statements
made by some of those who were connected with
me. I fear it has been stated by some of them
that I have induced them to join me, but the
contrary is true. I do not say this to injure them,
but regretting their weakness. Not one joined
me but of his own accord, and the greater part
at their own expense. A number of them I never
saw, and never had a word of conversation with,
till the day they came to me, and that was for
the purpose I have stated. Now, I have done.

HIS TONE AND MANNER.

Brown's speech was delivered in a calm, slow,
unfaltering voice, with no attempt at effect. A
correspondent of the *Herald* says : —

His composure, and his quiet and truthful manner while bearing testimony to the great indulgence that had been extended to him by the Court, throughout the whole of the proceedings, won the sympathy of every mind present. When he concluded, he quietly sat down.

In a moment after, he was escorted back to the prison, for the first time followed by the sympathy of the people, who gazed upon him with pitying eyes.

His counsel have put in a bill of exceptions, which will be referred to the Court of Appeals at Richmond.

HIS SENTENCE.

While Mr. Brown was speaking, perfect quiet prevailed; and when he had finished the judge proceeded to pronounce sentence upon him. After a few preliminary remarks, he said that no reasonable doubt could exist of the guilt of the prisoner; and sentenced him to be hung in public on Friday, the 2nd of December next.

Mr. Brown received his sentence with composure.

The only demonstration made was the clapping of the hands of one man in the crowd, who is not a resident of Jefferson County. This was promptly suppressed, and much regret was expressed by the citizens at its occurrence.

JOHN BROWN IN PRISON.

A lady, who visited Charlestown to assist Mrs. Lydia Maria Child, obtained two interviews with John Brown, the first of an hour, and the other for a shorter period.

Mrs.——, on entering, found Captain Brown lying on a cot, and Stephens on a large bed, Captain Brown arose from his bed to receive his guests, and stood a few moments leaning against the bedstead, immediately lying down again from weakness. His visitors were struck with the cheerfulness of his expression, and the calmness of his manner. He seemed not only passively resigned to his fate, but cheerful under it, and more than willing to meet it.

She said to him, " I expected Mrs. Child would be here to introduce me ; I am sorry not to find her, for her presence would make this room brighter for you."

He smiled, and replied, " I have written to her the reasons why she should not come ; but she was very kind—very kind !"

7

Some questions were then asked as to the treatment and care he had received ; to which he said, "I wish it to be understood by every body that I have been very kindly attended ; for if I had been under the care of father or brother, I could not have been better treated than by Captain Avis and his family."

HIS STATE OF MIND.

Mrs.—— had carried with her into the jail a large bunch of autumn leaves, gathered in the morning from the woods. There was no nail on the wall to hang them by, and she arranged them between the grated bars of the window. She gave to the sufferer a full-blown rose, which he laid beside his cheek on his pillow. The old man seemed to be greatly touched with these tokens of thoughtfulness. He is said to have always been a great lover of nature, particularly of the grandeur of forest scenes.

Mrs. —— drew a chair near his bedside, and taking out her knitting, sat by him for an hour. She has preserved his complete conversation, of which I can give only a small portion. She says : "I never saw a person who seemed less troubled or excited, or whose mind was less disturbed and more clear. His remarks are pointed, pithy, and sensible. He is not in the least sentimental, and seems to have singularly excellent common sense about every thing."

HIS PRINCIPLES ON SLAVERY.

She asked him the direct question,—"Were you actuated, in any degree, in undertaking your late enterprise, by a feeling of revenge?" adding that a common impression to that effect had gone abroad.

He manifested much surprise at this statement, and after pausing a moment, replied: "I am not conscious of ever having had a feeling of revenge; no, not in all the wrong done to me and my family in Kansas. But I can see that a thing is wrong and wicked, and can help to right it, and can even hope that those who do the wrong may be punished, and still have no feeling of revenge. No, I have not been actuated by any spirit of revenge."

He talked a good deal about his family, manifesting solicitude for their comfort after he was gone, but expressing his great confidence and trust in God's kind providence in their behalf.

When some allusion was made to the sentence which he had received, he said, very deliberately and firmly, and as my friend says, almost sub-

limely : " I do not think I can better serve the
cause I love so much than to die for it !"

She says that she can never forget the impres-
sive manner in which he uttered these solemn
words.   She replied : " It is not the hardest thing
than can happen to a brave man to die ; but it
must be a great hardship for an active man to
lie on his back in prison, disabled by wounds.
Do you not dread your confinement, and are you
not afraid that it may wear you down, or cause
you to relax your convictions, or regret your
attempt, or make your courage fail ?"

" I can not tell," he replied, "what weakness
may come over me ; but I do not think that I
shall deny my Lord and Master Jesus Christ, as
I certainly should, if I denied my principles
against slavery."

When the conversation had proceeded thus
far, as it was known outside the jail that a
Northern lady was inside, a crowd began to
collect, and although no demonstration of violence was made, yet there were manifest indications of impatience ; so that the sheriff called to
the jailer, and the jailer was obliged to put an
end to the interview.

BROWN'S INTERVIEW WITH HIS WIFE.

Mrs. Brown arrived at Charlestown, Dec. 1, to see her husband. The interview between them lasted from four o'clock in the afternoon until near eight o'clock in the evening, when General Tallaferro informed them that the period allowed had elapsed, and that she must prepare for departure to the Ferry. Capt. Brown urged that his wife be allowed to remain with him all night. To this the General refused to assent, allowing them but four hours.

The interview was not a very affecting one— rather of a practical character, with regard to the future of herself and children, and the arrangement and settlement of business affairs They seemed considerably affected when they first met, and Mrs. Brown was for a few moments quite overcome, but Brown was as firm as a rock, and she soon recovered her composure. There was an impression that the prisoner might possibly be furnished with a weapon or with strychnine by his wife, and before the interview her person was searched by the wife of the jailer, and a strict watch kept over them during the time they were together.

On first meeting they kissed and affectionately embraced, and Mrs. Brown shed a few tears, but immediately checked her feelings. They stood embraced, and she sobbing, for nearly five minutes, and he was apparently unable to speak. The prisoner only gave way for a moment, and was soon calm and collected, and remained firm throughout the interview. At the close they shook hands, but did not embrace, and as they parted he said, " God bless you and the children !" Mrs. Brown replied, " God have mercy on you !" and continued calm until she left the room, when she remained in tears a few moments, and then prepared to depart. The interview took place in the parlour of Captain Avis, and the prisoner was free from manacles of any kind. They sat side by side on a sofa, and after discussing family matters proceeded to business.

THE EXECUTION OF BROWN.

At eleven o'clock on 2nd December, the prisoner was brought out of the jail, accompanied by Sheriff Campbell and assistants, and Captain Avis, the jailer. As he came out, the six companies of infantry and one troop of horse, with General Tallaferro, and his entire staff, were deploying in front of the jail, while an open waggon with a pine box, in which was a fine oak coffin, was waiting for him.

Brown looked around, and spoke to several persons he recognized, and, walking down the steps, took a seat on the coffin box along with the jailer, Avis. He looked with interest on the fine military display, but made no remarks. The waggon moved off, flanked by two files of riflemen in close order. On reaching the field the military had already full possession. Pickets were established, and the citizens kept back, at the point of the bayonet, from taking any position but that assigned them.

Brown was accompanied by no ministers, he desiring no religious services either in the jail or on the scaffold.

JOHN BROWN OF OSAWATOMIE.

JOHN BROWN, of Osawatomie,
  Spake on his dying day :
" I will not have, to shrive my soul,
  A priest in Slavery's pay ;
But, let some poor slave-mother,
  Whom I have striven to free,
With her children, from the gallows-stair,
  Put up a prayer for me !"

John Brown, of Osawatomie,
  They led him out to die,
When lo, a poor slave-mother,
  With her little child, pressed nigh.
Then the bold, blue eye grew tender,
  And the old, harsh face grew mild,
As he stooped between the jeering ranks
  And kissed the negro's child !— *Whittier.*

On reaching the field where the gallows was erected, the prisoner said, "Why, are none but military allowed in the inclosure? I am sorry citizens have been kept out." On reaching the gallows, he observed Mr. Hunter and Mayor Green standing near, to whom he said, "Gentlemen, good-by!" his voice not faltering.

ON THE GALLOWS.

The prisoner walked up the steps firmly, and was the first man on the gallows. Avis and Sheriff Campbell stood by his side, and after shaking hands and bidding an affectionate adieu, he thanked them for their kindness, when the cap was put over his face, and the rope around his neck. Avis asked him to step forward on the trap. He replied, "You must lead me, I can not see." The rope was adjusted, and the military order given, "Not ready yet." The soldiers marched, countermarched, and took position as if any enemy were in sight, and were thus occupied for nearly ten minutes, the prisoner standing all the time. Avis inquired if he was not tired. Brown said, "No, not tired; but don't keep me waiting longer than is necessary.

While on the scaffold Sheriff Campbell asked him if he would take a handkerchief in his hand to drop as a signal when he was ready. He replied, " No, I do not want it ; but do not detain me any longer than is absolutely necessary."

He was swung off at fifteen minutes past eleven. A slight grasping of the hands and twitching of the muscles were seen, and then all was quiet.

The body was several times examined, and the pulse did not cease until thirty-five minutes had passed. The body was then cut down, placed in a coffin, and conveyed under military escort to the depot, where it was put in a car to be carried to the ferry by a special train at four o'clock.

JOHN BROWN'S AUTOGRAPH.

One of the jail-guard, a worthy gentleman of this place, asked of Captain Brown his autograph, He expressed the kindest feeling for him, and said he would give it upon this consideration— that he should not make a speculation out of it. The gentleman never alluded to the subject again, but on the morning of execution Brown sent for him, and handed him the following communication :—

CHARLESTOWN, Va.,
December, 2nd, 1859.

I, John Brown, am now quite *certain* that the crimes of this *guilty land* will never be purged *away* but with *blood*. I had, as I now think, vainly flattered myself that, without much blood-shed, it might be done.

VICTOR HUGO ON JOHN BROWN.

The following is part of an address which has been published :—

When we reflect on what Brown, the liberator, the champion of Christ, has striven to effect, and when we remember that he is about to die, slaughtered by the American Republic, the crime assumes the proportions of the nation which commits it ; and when we say to our-selves that this nation is a glory of the human race ; that—like France, like England, like Ger-many—she is one of the organs of civilization ; that she sometimes even outmarches Europe by the sublime audacity of her progress ; that she is the queen of an entire world ; and that she bears on her brow an immense light of freedom, we affirm that John Brown will not die, for we recoil, horror-struck, from the idea of so great a crime committed by so great a people.

In a political light, the murder of Brown would be an irreparable fault. It would pene-trate the Union with a secret fissure, which would in the end tear it asunder. It is possible that the execution of Brown might consolidate slavery in Virginia, but it is certain that it would convulse the entire American democracy. You preserve your shame, but you sacrifice your glory.

In a moral light, it seems to me that a portion of the light of humanity would be eclipsed—that even the idea of justice and injustice would be obscured on the day which should witness the assassination of emancipation by liberty.

As for myself, though I am but an atom, yet being, as I am, in common with all other men, inspired with the conscience of humanity, I kneel in tears before the great starry banner of the New World, and with clasped hands, and with profound and filial respect, I implore the illustrious American republic, sister of the French republic, to look to the safety of the universal moral law, to save Brown, to throw down the threatening scaffold of the 16th of December, and not to suffer, beneath its eyes, and I add, with a shudder, almost by its fault, the first fratricide be outdone.

For—yes, let America know it, and ponder it well—there is something more terrible than Cain slaying Abel—it is Washington slaying Sparticus.

VICTOR HUGO.

Hauteville House, Dec. 2, 1859.

JOHN BROWN SONG.

John Brown died on a scaffold for the slave ;
Dark was the hour when we dug his hallowed **grave ;**
Now God avenges the life he gladly gave,—
  Freedom reigns to-day !
   Glory, glory, hallelujah,
   Glory, glory, hallelujah,
   Glory, glory, hallelujah,
  Freedom reigns to-day !

John Brown sowed, and his harvesters are **we ;**
Honour to him who has made the bondmen **free !**
Loved ever more shall our noble ruler be ;
  Freedom reigns to-day !
   Glory, glory, hallelujah,
   Glory, &c.

John Brown's body lies mouldering in the **grave ;**
Bright, o'er the sod, let the starry banner **wave ;**
Lo ! for the millions he perilled all to save,
  Freedom reigns to-day !
   Glory, &c.

John Brown's soul through the world is marching **on ;**
Hail to the hour when oppression shall be gone !
All men will sing, in the better ages' dawn,
  Freedom reigns to-day.
   Glory, &c.

John Brown dwells where the battle-strife is o'er ;
Hate cannot harm him, nor sorrow stir him **more ;**
Earth will remember the martyrdom he bore ;
  Freedom reigns to-day !
   Glory, &c.

John Brown's body lies mouldering in the grave ;
John Brown lives in the triumphs of the brave ;
John Brown's soul not a higher joy can crave ;
      Freedom reigns to-day !
            Glory, glory, hallelujah !
            Glory, glory, hallelujah !
            Glory, glory, hallelujah !
      Freedom reigns to-day !

                        —*Edna A. Proctor.*

CHAPTER IV.

AT WORK IN KENTUCKY.

 FEW months after the death of John Brown, I felt impelled to go again into the land of darkness and slavery, and make another effort to help the oppressed to freedom. This time I decided to make Kentucky my field of labour. I consequently went to Louisville, where I remained for a few days looking about for a suitable locality for my work. I finally decided, to go down to Harrodsburg, in the character of one in search of a farm. Securing a few letters from land agents in Louisville, introducing me as Mr. Hawkins, of Canada, I reached Harrodsburg in due time. After a little enquiry, I learned that a Mr. B——, five miles from that place, had a very desirable farm for sale. Securing a conveyance, I was driven out to Mr. B——'s, who received me in a friendly manner, when he learned that I was in search of a farm, and invited me

to remain with him while I was in the neighbourhood. I accepted his invitation, and sent the
conveyance back to Harrodsburg. Mr. B——'s
family consisted of himself, wife, and three
small children. He was the owner of the
farm on which he lived, consisting of three
hundred acres. He also owned eleven slave
men and women, and several slave children.
He informed me that he had concluded to sell
his farm and stock, except the human chattels,
and remove to Texas. During our frequent
conversations upon the subject of land, stock,
climate, soil, etc., I seized every opportunity,
especially if any of the slaves were near, to
allude to Canada in favourable terms. I did
not fail to observe the quiet but deep interest
evinced by the slaves in our conversations. On
the third day of my visit, our negotiations about
the farm were approaching—what Mr. B——
considered—a favourable conclusion, when he
casually informed me that his title-deeds were
in Frankfort, and that, if I was in other respects
pleased with the farm, he would go to Frankfort and bring the deeds for my inspection. I
expressed my satisfaction with the farm, and
told him I thought he had better bring the
deeds that I might look them over. On the
following morning he left for Frankfort. Before
leaving, I asked him to allow one of the slaves

to accompany me to the woods, while I amused myself gunning. He replied that I might take any of them I pleased. I selected a bright, intelligent looking mulatto, whom I had frequently noticed listening most attentively to my conversation with his master. When we reached the woods, he begged and implored me to buy him and take him to Canada.

A WIFE TORN FROM HER HUSBAND AND SOLD.

He told me that his master had sold his wife, to whom he had been married only a month, to a hotel-keeper in Covington, he spoke of his deep love for her; that his master was going to take him to Texas, and that he should never see her again. The tears rolled down the poor fellow's cheeks in streams. I told him to cheer up; that I would do my best to liberate him. I then confided to him the object that brought me there; and told him that if liberty was precious to him he must prepare to make great efforts and sacrifices for it. I explained to him that if he could reach Cincinnati, Ohio, he would be safe from his pursuers, and that he would be sheltered and protected until he reached Canada. I then gave him the address of a friend in Cincinnati on whom he could rely for protection, and also furnished him with some money, a pistol, and pocket-compass for the journey to the Ohio. When he took the pistol in his hand, I charged him not to use it except to prevent his capture. He grasped the pistol like a vice, and said, "Massa, I'll get to Cincinnati, if I am not killed." I then asked him if any of the other slaves were capable of undertaking the journey. For a moment he was silent, thinking, then he replied, " No, massa ; they are bad niggers ; don't you trust dem." I advised him to work on faithfully until Saturday night—it was now Wednesday—and to make every preparation to leave at midnight on that day, and to travel by night only. I told him I should go direct to Covington on Friday, and would endeavour to liberate his wife ; that, if I succeeded, he would find her at the house of the same friend in Cincinnati, whose address I had given him. I advised him to carry with him as much food as possible, so as to avoid exposure while on his journey. Poor Peter was nearly wild with his prospects; so much so, indeed, that I urged him to repress his feelings, for fear his conduct would be noticed by his mistress, who had imbibed a particular dislike to Peter since his separation from his wife. Mrs. B—— told me he was a wicked nigger ; that ever since Mr. B—— had sold the *gal,* Peter had looked gloomy and revengeful ; that she hated him. Mrs. B—— could not understand that Peter had any right,

8

not even the right to sorrow, when his wife was
torn from him and sold to a stranger.

On Thursday, Mr. B—— returned. He had
been unsuccessful in obtaining the deeds, and
told me that his lawyers in Louisville, were
willing I should have every facility to examine
them in their office, if I pleased ; but, as they
held a small mortgage on the property, they
were unwilling to permit the deeds to go out
of their possession. This was very satisfactory,
and afforded me an opportunity to get away
without creating suspicion. During the night,
previous to my departure, I obtained an interview with Peter, and reiterated my injunctions
to be brave, cautious, and persevering, while on
the journey, and again impressed upon his
memory my instructions. Poor fellow ! his eyes
filled with tears when I told him I was going
direct to Covington next day, and should try and
free his wife. When I bid him good-bye, he
frantically kissed my hand, saying, "Tell Polly
I'll be dere, sure. Tell her to wait for me."

Oh ! what a vile, wicked institution was that
which could make merchandise of such a man
as stood before me ! Yet, monstrous and cruel
as it was, it had its apologists and abettors
in the North ; while from every pulpit in the

Slave States went forth the declaration, that "slavery was a wise and beneficent institution, devised by God for the protection of an inferior race."

On Friday morning I left, ostensibly for Louisville, but went to Covington, which place I reached on the following day. I had no difficulty in finding the hotel, having got the name of Polly's owner from Peter. It was a poorly kept hostelry; the proprietor evidently had no knowledge of hotel-keeping. I however took quarters with him, and found him a very communicative man. He informed me he had been a farmer until within a year past, but finding that farming on a small scale was unprofitable, he had sold out, and bought this hotel. He was the owner of two negroes, a man and woman; "the gal was *likely*, but mighty spunky." He had paid twelve hundred dollars for her to Mr. B——, near Harrodsburg. He wanted her to "take up" with his negro boy, but she refused. He had threatened to send her to New Orleans for sale, if she would not obey him. He *reckoned* she would be glad to "take up" with him before long; a good whipping generally brought them to their senses. He knew how to manage *such*. The gal would bring sixteen hundred or two thousand dollars in New Orleans, because she was *likely*.

Before retiring that night, I requested the landlord to send to my room some warm water for
a bath. He said he would send the girl up
with it as soon as it was ready. In less than half
an hour, the water was placed in my room by a
bright, intelligent, straight-haired mulatto girl,
apparently twenty years of age. As soon as she
entered the room, I directed her to close the
door, and said in a whisper, "Are you Polly,
from Harrodsburg?" She looked at me with a
frightened look, "Yes, massa, I is," she said. I
told her I had seen her husband, Peter, and that
he was going to run away from his master on
Sunday night; that I had friends in Cincinnati
where he was going, who would secrete him until
she could join him, when they would both be
sent to Canada. She stood like a statue, while
I was talking. I directed her to get ready to
meet me on the following night, at twelve o'clock,
in front of the post office; that I should leave
the hotel in the morning and make preparations
to have her taken across the river to the Ohio
shore. She was so much amazed that for a moment she was unable to speak; at last she said,
"Please, massa, tell me it over again." I repeated my instructions as rapidly as possible for
fear I should be interrupted; and warned her
against betraying herself by any outward expression of her feelings. When I concluded, she

said, " Oh, massa, I'll pray to God for you—I'll
be dere sure." She then left the room. Next
morning I delayed coming down to breakfast
until after the regular breakfast was over, hoping
to obtain another opportunity of charging her
memory with the instructions already given.
I was fortunate—she served the table. When
I was leaving the table, I said to her, " *To-night,
at twelve o'clock, sure.*" She replied in a whisper,
" God will help me, massa, I'll try to." After
breakfast, I went to Cincinnati and with the
aid of friends, made arrangements to cross to
Covington at eleven o'clock that night.

LIBERATION OF THE WIFE.

Before dark on Sunday evening, I had completed all my arrangements. A short time before midnight, I crossed the river in a small boat
with two good assistants. Leaving them in
charge of the boat, I went up to the post office,
which I reached a few minutes before twelve.
I waited patiently for nearly half an hour, when
I observed a dark object approaching rapidly at
a distance of several hundred yards from where
I stood. As soon as I recognized the form, I
went toward her, and, telling her to follow me,
I turned down a dark street, and went toward
the river. We had made but little progress

before we were stopped by a night watchman, who said, "Where are you going?" I replied by putting a dollar in his hand and saying, it's all right. He became oblivious, and passed on his beat, greatly to my peace of mind. We soon reached the boat ; she crouched down in the bow, and we left the Kentucky shore.

CROSSING THE OHIO.

In a short time we were safe across the river, and placing my charge in a cab which I had ready at the shore, we drove rapidly up into the city within a few blocks of my friend's residence. I then dismissed the cab, and we wended our way through several streets, until I reached the rear entrance to the house of my friend. We were admitted, and received the kind attention of our generous and liberty-loving host. Poor Polly, who had never before been treated with such kindness, said to me : "Massa, is I free now?" I told her she was now free from her master ; and that, as soon as her husband arrived, they both would be sent to Cleveland, where I would meet them, and help them across to Canada, where they would be as free as the whites. Bidding her and my noble hearted friend good-by, I took the first train on Monday morning for Cleveland. On my arrival there, I drove a few

miles into the country to the house of a friend
of the cause, where I remained waiting for news
of Peter's arrival in Cincinnati. On Friday
morning I received a letter informing me that
Peter had arrived safely, though his feet were
torn and sore. The meeting between husband
and wife was described as most affecting. On
Monday evening following, I received another
letter stating that freight car No. 705, had been
hired to convey a box containing one "package of
hardware," and one of "dry goods," to Cleveland.
The letter also contained the key of the car.
The train containing this particular car was to
leave Cincinnati on Tuesday morning, and would
reach Cleveland, sometime during the evening of
the same day. I had but a short time consequently to make preparations to convey the
fugitives across the lake.

A KENTUCKIAN IN SEARCH OF HIS CHATTEL.

On Tuesday morning, my good friend with
whom I had been stopping, drove me into Cleveland. As we passed the American House, I
caught sight of my Kentucky host standing in
front of the hotel. He did not observe me,
however, and we continued on our way to the
lake shore. I then sent my friend back to make
the acquaintance of the Kentuckian, and learn

the object of his visit to Cleveland. After a
long search, I found a schooner loading for Port
Stanley, Canada. The skipper said they would
be ready to sail on the following day if the
wind was favourable. I soon learned that the
captain was a Freemason, and confided to him
my secret. The result was, his agreement to
stow my freight away safely as soon as they
came on board, and carry them to Canada I
then returned to a locality agreed upon with
my friend, whom I found waiting for me, and was
then driven to the country. On the way out,
my friend informed me that he had made the
acquaintance of the Kentuckian, who felt very
sore over the loss of his slave ; but he did not
express any suspicion of me. He said he was
having posters printed, offering a reward of five
hundred dollars for the capture of the girl.
Toward night, I again went into the city, and
my friend made enquiry at the freight office of
the railroad, and ascertained that the train
containing car 705, would be in at 10 p.m. We
then went to a hotel near the depot, and
remained until the train came. I found the
car, and my faithful friend brought his carriage
as near as he could safely, without attracting
attention. I unlocked the door of the car, went
in, and closed the door after me. Listening
carefully, I could not detect the slightest signs

of life in the car. I called in a low voice:
"Peter." A reply came at once: "Yes, massa,
shall I open the box?" The two poor creatures
were in a dry-goods box, sufficiently large
to permit them to sit upright. I helped them
out of the box, and making sure that no
stranger was near, opened the door of the
car, and led them quickly to the carriage.
We then drove rapidly away to the boat, and
secreted the fugitives in the cabin. I then bid my
friend farewell, as I had decided not to leave the
two faithful creatures until they were safe in
Canada.

SAFE ARRIVAL OF MAN AND WIFE IN CANADA.

After midnight the breeze freshened up, and
we made sail for the land of freedom. We had
a rough and tedious voyage, and did not reach
Canada until near night on the following day.
When our little vessel was safely moored along-
side the pier, I led my two companions on shore,
and told them they were now in a land where
freedom was guaranteed to all. And we kneeled
together on the soil of Canada, and thanked
the Almighty Father for his aid and protection. Two happier beings I never saw. Next
day I took them to London, and obtained situa-
tions for both Peter and his wife. I succeeded

also in enlisting the kind interest of several prominent persons in their behalf, to whom I related their experience.

NET RESULTS.

The next three months I spent in Canada, visiting those refugees in whom I had taken a personal interest. I found six in Chatham, two in London, four in Hamilton, two in Amherstburg, and one in Toronto—fifteen in all; while several others had gone from Canada to New England.

It afforded me great satisfaction to find them sober, industrious members of society. It has often been remarked by both Canadians and visitors from the States, that the negro refugees in Canada were superior specimens of their race. The observation is true, for none but superior specimens could hope to reach Canada. The difficulties and dangers of the route, and the fact that they were often closely followed for weeks, not only by human foes, but by bloodhounds as well, required the exercise of rare qualities of mind and body. Their route would often lay through dismal swamps inhabited only by wild animals and poisonous reptiles. Sometimes the distance between the land of bondage and freedom was several hundreds of miles, every mile of which had to be traversed on foot. It is, indeed, surprising that so large a number of fugitives succeeded in reaching Canada, considering the obstacles they had to contend with on their long and dangerous journey.

When I reflect upon the dangers that surrounded me during that stormy period, I acknowledge my indebtedness to God for His protection and support during my labours in behalf of the oppressed people of the Southern States; and, although the results of my efforts were insignificant in comparison to what I hoped to accomplish when I began the work in 1855, I still rejoice that I was enabled to do what little I did for the poor and despised coloured people of the Slave States.

NUMBER OF REFUGEE NEGROES IN CANADA.

The number of refugee negroes living in Canada, at the outbreak of the slaveholder's rebellion, was not far short of forty thousand. Probably more than half of them were manumitted slaves who, in consequence of unjust laws, were compelled to leave the States where they were manumitted. Many of these negroes settled in the Northern States, but the greater portion of them came to Canada.

THE FUGITIVE SLAVE LAW.

When the Fugitive Slave Law was enacted in 1850, it carried terror to every person of African blood, in the Free States. Stung with hopeless despair, more than six thousand Christian men and women fled from their homes, and sought refuge under the flag of Britain in Canada. In the words of Charles Sumner : " The Free States became little better than a huge outlying plantation, quivering under the lash of the overseer ; or rather they were a diversified hunting ground for the flying bondman, resounding always with the ' halloo' of the huntsman. There seemed to be no rest. The chase was hardly finished at Boston, before it broke out at Philadelphia, Syracuse, or Buffalo, and then again raged furiously over the prairies of the west. Not a case occurred which did not shock the conscience of the country, and sting it with anger. The records of the time attest the accuracy of this statement. Perhaps there is no instance in history where human passion showed itself in grander forms of expression, or where eloquence lent all her gifts more completely to the demands of liberty, than the speech of Theodore Parker, (now dead and buried in a foreign land), denouncing the capture of Thomas Simms at Boston, and invoking the judgment of God and man upon the agents in

this wickedness. The great effort cannot be forgotten in the history of humanity. But every
case pleaded with an eloquence of its own, until
at last one of those tragedies occurred which
darken the heavens, and cry out with a voice that
will be heard. It was the voice of a mother
standing over her murdered child. Margaret
Garner had escaped from slavery with three
children, but she was overtaken at Cincinnati.
Unwilling to see her offspring returned to the
shambles of the South, this unhappy person,
described in the testimony as 'a womanly,
amiable, affectionate mother,' determined to
save them in the only way within her power.
With a butcher knife, coolly and deliberately,
she took the life of one of the children, described
as 'almost white, and a little girl of rare beauty,'
and attempted, without success, to take the life
of the other two. To the preacher who interrogated her, she exclaimed: 'The child is my
own, given me of God to do the best a mother
could in its behalf. I have done the best I
could; I would have done more and better for
the rest; I knew it was better for them to go
home to God than back to slavery.' But she
was restrained in her purpose. The Fugitive
Slave Act triumphed, and after the determination of sundry questions of jurisdiction, this
devoted historic mother, with the two children

that remained to her, and the dead body of the little one just emancipated, was escorted by a national guard of armed men to the doom of slavery. But her case did not end with this revolting sacrifice. So long as the human heart is moved by human suffering, the story of this mother will be read with alternate anger and grief, while it is studied as a perpetual witness to the slaveholding tyranny which then ruled the Republic with execrable exactions, destined at last to break out in war, as the sacrifice of Virginia by her father is a perpetual witness to the decemviral tyranny which ruled Rome. But liberty is always priceless. There are other instances less known in which kindred wrong has been done. Every case was a tragedy—under the forms of law. Worse than poisoned bowl or dagger was the certificate of a United States commissioner—who was allowed, without interruption, to continue his dreadful trade."

THE PRESIDENTIAL ELECTION OF 1860.

During no previous presidential election, (except that of 1856, when Fremont and Buchanan were the candidates), was there so much excitement on the slavery question as that of 1860, when Lincoln, Breckinridge, Bell, and Douglas were the candidates.

To enable my readers to form a correct idea
as to the political positions occupied by the
different candidates towards the institution of
slavery, I give below the "slavery plank of each
platform" on which the presidential candidates
went before the people for their suffrages :—

REPUBLICAN NATIONAL (LINCOLN) PLATFORM.

ADOPTED AT CHICAGO, 1860.

Resolved, That we, the delegated representatives of the
Republican electors of the United States, in Convention
assembled, in discharge of the duty we owe to our constituents
and our country, unite in the following declarations :—

1. That the history of the nation, during the last four years,
has fully established the propriety and necessity of the organization and perpetuation of the Republican party, and that
the causes which called it into existence are permanent in
their nature, and now, more than ever before, demand its
peaceful and constitutional triumph.

2. That the maintenance of the principles promulgated in
the Declaration of Independence and embodied in the Federal
Constitution, "That all men are created equal; that they are
endowed by their creator with certain inalienable rights ; that
among these are life, liberty, and the pursuit of happiness ;
that to secure these rights, goverments are instituted among
men, deriving their just powers from the consent of the
governed," is essential to the preservation of our Republican
institutions ; and that the Federal Constitution, the Rights of
the States, and the Union of the States, must and shall be
preserved.

7. That the new dogma, that the Constitution, of its own
force, carries Slavery into any or all of the Territories of the
United States, is a dangerous political heresy, at variance
with the explicit provisions of that instrument itself, with
contemporaneous exposition, and with legislative and judicial
precedent ; is revolutionary in its tendency, and subversive of
the peace and harmony of the country.

8. That the normal condition of all the territory of the United States is that of freedom ; That as our Republican fathers, when they had abolished Slavery in all our national territory, ordained that "no person should be deprived of life, liberty, or property, without due process of law," it becomes our duty, by legislation, whenever such legislation is necessary, to maintin this provision of the Constitution against all attempts to violate it ; and we deny the authority of Congress, of a territorial legislature, or of any individuals, to give legal existence to Slavery in any Territory of the United States.

9. That we brand the recent re-opening of the African slave-trade, under the cover of our national flag, aided by perversions of judicial power, as a crime against humanity and a burning shame to our country and age ; and we call upon Congress to take prompt and efficient measures for the total and final suppression of that execrable traffic.

NATIONAL DEMOCRATIC (DOUGLAS) PLATFORM.

Adopted at Charleston and Baltimore, 1860.

1. *Resolved*, That we, the Democracy of the Union, in Convention assembled, hereby declare our affirmance of the following resolutions :—

Resolved, That the enactments of State Legislatures to defeat the faithful execution of the Fugitive Slave Law, are hostile in character, subversive of the Constitution, and revolutionary in their effect.

Resolved, That it is in accordance with the true interpretation of the Cincinnati Platform, that, during the existence of the Territorial Governments, the measure of restriction, whatever it may be, imposed by the Federal Constitution on the power of the Territorial Legislature over the subject of the domestic relations, as the same has been, or shall hereafter be, finally determined by the Supreme Court of the United States, shall be respected by all good citizens, and enforced with promptness and fidelity by every branch of the General Government.

NATIONAL DEMOCRATIC (BRECKINRIDGE) PLATFORM.

ADOPTED AT CHARLESTON AND BALTIMORE, 1860.

Resolved, That the Platform adopted by the Democratic party at Cincinnati be affirmed, with the following explanatory Resolutions :—

1. That the Government of a Territory organized by an Act of Congress, is provisional and temporary ; and during its existence, all citizens of the United States have an equal right to settle with their property in the Territory, without their rights, either of person or property, being destroyed or impaired by Congressional or Territorial legislation.

2. That it is the duty of the Federal Government, in all its departments, to protect, when necessary, the rights of persons and property in the Territories, and wherever else its constitutional authority extends.

3. That when the settlers in a Territory having an adequate population, form a State Constitution, in pursuance of law, the right of sovereignty commences, and, being consummated by admission into the Union, they stand on an equal footing with the people of other States ; and the State thus organized ought to be admitted into the Federal Union, whether its Constitution prohibits or recognizes the institution of Slavery.

5. That the enactments of State Legislatures to defeat the faithful execution of the Fugitive Slave Law are hostile in character, subversive of the Constitution, and revolutionary in their effect.

CONSTITUTIONAL UNION (BELL-EVERETT) PLATFORM.

ADOPTED AT BALTIMORE, 1860.

Whereas, Experience has demonstrated that Platforms adopted by the partisan conventions of the country have had the effect to mislead and deceive the people, and at the same time to widen the political divisions of the country, by the creation and encouragement of geographical and sectional parties ; therefore,

9

Resolved, That it is both the part of patriotism and of duty *to recognize* no political principle other than THE CONSTITUTION OF THE COUNTRY, THE UNION OF THE STATES, AND THE EN- FORCEMENT OF THE LAWS, and that as representatives of the Constitutional Union men of the country in National Conven- tion assembled, we hereby pledge ourselves to obtain, protect, and defend, separately and unitedly, these great principles of public liberty and national safety, against all enemies at home and abroad, believing that thereby peace may once more be restored to the country, the rights of the People and of the States re-established, and the Government again placed in that condition, of justice, fraternity, and equality, which under the example and Constitution of our fathers, has solemnly bound every citizen of the United States to maintain a more perfect union, establish justice, insure domestic tran- quility, provide for the common defence, promote the general welfare, and secure the blessings of liberty to ourselves and our posterity.

ELECTORAL VOTE, PRESIDENTAL ELECTION OF 1860.

For Lincoln and Hamlin 180
For Breckinridge and Lane 72
For Bell and Everett 39
For Douglas and Johnson 12

Whole Electoral Vote................... 303

Lincoln's majority over all... 57

When enough returns from the election had been received to render it certain that Abraham Lincoln would be the next President, public meetings were held in the city of Charleston and in other places in the State of South Carolina, at which resolutions were adopted in favor of the Secession of the State from the Union.

DECLARATION OF INDEPENDENCE OF SOUTH CAROLINA.

DONE IN CONVENTION, DECEMBER 24, 1860.

The State of South Carolina, having determined to resume her separate and equal place among nations, deems it due to herself, to the remaining United States of America, and to the nations of the world, that she should declare the causes which have led to this act.

We affirm that these ends for which this government was instituted have been defeated, and the government itself has been made destructive of them by the action of the non-slave-holding States. These States have assumed the right of deciding upon the propriety of our domestic institutions, and have denied the rights of property established in fifteen of the States and recognized by the Constitution; they have denounced as sinful the institution of slavery; they have permitted the open establishment among them of societies whose avowed object is to disturb the peace and to eloin the property of the citizens of other States. They have encouraged and assisted thousands of our slaves to leave their homes, and those who remain have been incited by emissaries to servile insurrection.

Sectional interest and animosity will deepen the irritation, and all hope of remedy is rendered vain by the fact that public opinion at the north has invested a great political error with the sanctions of a more erroneous religious belief.

We, therefore, the people of South Carolina, appealing to the Supreme Judge of the world for the rectitude of our intentions, have solemnly declared that the union heretofore existing between this State and the other States of North America is dissolved, and that the State of South Carolina has resumed her position among the nations of the world as a free, sovereign, and independent State.

And for the support of this declaration, with a firm reliance on the protection of Divine Providence, we mutually pledge to each other our lives, our fortunes, and our sacred honor.

On the same day the remaining representatives in Congress from South Carolina vacated their seats and returned home; and thus began the slaveholders' rebellion.

CHAPTER V.

THE SLAVEHOLDERS' REBELLION.

FOR many months after the death of John Brown, I felt that the defeat of his plans at Harper's Ferry was a great calamity to the enslaved. I saw nothing in store for them but toil and bondage for another generation. For who, at that time, foresaw the mighty conflict that was soon to be inaugurated by the haughty slaveholders, in which they and their cherished institution were to be completely overthrown.

The seed sown at Harper's Ferry, had fallen into rich soil. The slaveholders were convinced that unless they could obtain from the North further guarantees for the protection of the institution of slavery—that secession from the Free States was their only salvation. Their insolent demands upon the North were met by a quiet determination upon the part of the people ; that not another foot of the public domain should be given up to slavery. Northern politicians had become so accustomed to yielding obedience to the commands of the slave drivers, that strong efforts were made to effect a compromise with the pro-slavery leaders in Congress.

But the patience of the peace-loving people of the Free States, was at length exhausted; they had submitted to the outrageous provisions of the Fugitive Slave Law ; they had looked on and seen the champions of freedom in Congress insulted and assaulted by the slave drivers of the South ; they had borne for years the taunts and sneers of the Southern chivalry ; and now, they resolved to assert their just rights and privileges as citizens of a free country.

The threats and demands of the slaveholders were treated with the contempt they deserved.

CONFIDENTIAL SERVICE IN CANADA.

A few months after the inauguration of President Lincoln, I received a letter from a friend in Washington, requesting me to visit him at my very earliest convenience ; that he desired to confer with me on a subject of importance.

The day after my arrival in Washington, my friend introduced me to the President. Mr. Lincoln received me very cordially, and invited me to dine with him that day. Assembled at the President's table were several prominent gentlemen, to whom Mr. Lincoln introduced me as "a red-hot abolitionist from Canada."

One of the guests, a prominent member of Congress (severely injured in after years by coming in contact with the *Credit Mobilier*), remarked, in a slurring manner, that he wished all the negroes of the United States would emigrate to Canada, as we Canadians were so fond of them. Mr. Lincoln said : "It would be all the better for the negroes, that's certain."

"Yes," I replied, a little warmly, "it would be all the better for the negroes ; for, under our flag, the blackest negro is entitled to, and freely accorded every right and privilege enjoyed by native Canadians. We make no distinction in respect to the colour of a man's skin. It is true, we live under a monarchial form of government ; but, under that government, every man, and woman, whether white, black, or brown, have equal rights before our laws."

Mr. Lincoln, in a jocular way, said to the member of Congress, "If you are not careful, you will bring on a war with Canada. I think we have got a big enough job on hand now."

The conversation then turned on the attitude of England toward the Free States in their contest with the slaveholders. One gentleman remarked that he was surprised to see so many manifestations of unfriendliness on the part of the English and Canadian people, and asked me how I accounted for it. I replied, "How can you expect it otherwise, when there exists in the Northern States so wide a diversity of opinion as to the justness of your cause ? The unfriendly expressions of an English statesman, or the avowed sympathy of a few English and Canadian papers, are noted by you with painful surprise ; while the treasonable utterances and acts of some of your own political leaders and people are quite overlooked. Besides, you cannot expect the sympathy of the Christian world in your behalf, while you display such an utter disregard for the rights and liberties of your own citizens, as I witnessed in this city yesterday."

Mr. Lincoln asked what I alluded to. I replied, " A United States Marshall passed through Washington yesterday, having in his charge a coloured man, who he was taking over to Virginia under the provisions of your Fugitive Slave

Law. The man had escaped from his master—
who is an open rebel—and fled to Wilmington,
Delaware, where he was arrested, and taken
back into slavery."

After dinner, Mr. Lincoln led me to a window,
distant from the rest of the party, and said,
" Mr. S. sent for you at my request. We need
a confidential person in Canada to look after
the rebel emissaries there, and keep us posted
as to their schemes and objects. You have
been strongly recommended to me for the position. Your mission shall be as confidential as
you please. No one here but your friend Mr. S.
and myself, shall have any knowledge of your
position. Your communications may be sent
direct to me, under cover to Major ——. Think
it over to-night ; and if you can accept the mission, come up and see me at nine o'clock to-morrow morning." When I took my leave of him, he
said, " I hope you will decide to serve us."

The position thus offered, was one not suited
to my tastes or feelings, but, as Mr. Lincoln
appeared very desirous that I should accept it,
I concluded to lay aside my prejudices and
accept the responsibilities of the mission. I
was also persuaded to this conclusion by the
wishes of my friend.

At nine o'clock next morning, I waited upon the President, and announced my decision. He grasped my hand in a hearty manner, and said: "Thank you; thank you; I am glad of it."

I said: "Mr. Lincoln, if even *one* of the objects of your Government was the liberation from bondage of the poor slaves of the South, I would feel justified in accepting any position where I could best serve you, but when I see so much tenderness for that vile institution and for the interests of slaveholders, I almost doubt whether your efforts to crush the rebellion will meet with the favour of heaven."

He replied: "I sincerely wish that all men were free, and I especially wish for the complete abolition of slavery in this country; but my private wishes and feelings must yield to the necessities of my position. My first duty is, to maintain the integrity of the Union. With that object in view, I shall endeavour to save it, either with or without slavery. I have always been an anti-slavery man. Away back in 1839, when I was a member of the Legislature of Illinois, I presented a resolution asking for the emancipation of slavery in the District of Columbia, when, with but few exceptions, the popular mind of my State was opposed to it.

If the destruction of the institution of slavery should be one of the results of this conflict which the slaveholders have forced upon us, I shall rejoice as hearty as you. In the meantime, help us to circumvent the machinations of the rebel agents in Canada. There is no doubt they will use your country as a communicating link with Europe, and also with their friends in New York. It is quite possible also that they may make Canada a base, to annoy our people along the frontier. Keep us well posted of what they say and do."

After a lengthy conversation relative to private matters connected with my mission, I rose to leave, when he said: "I will walk down to 'Willards' with you, the hotel is on my way to the Capitol, where I have an engagement at noon."

Before we reached the hotel, a man came up to the President, and thrust a letter into his hand, at the same time applying for some office in Wisconsin. I saw that the President was offended at the rudeness, for he passed the letter back without looking at it, saying: "No, sir! I am not going to open shop here." This was said in a most emphatic manner, but accompanied by a comical gesture which caused the rejected applicant to smile. As we continued our walk, the President remarked on the annoyances incident to his position, saying : " These office-seekers are a curse to this country. No sooner was my election certain, than I became the prey of hundreds of hungry, persistent applicants for office, whose highest ambition is to feed at the government crib."

When he bid me good-bye, he said : " Let me hear from you once a week at least."

As he was about to leave me, a young army officer stopped him, and made some request, to which the President replied with a good deal of humour : " No ; I can't do that. I must not interfere : they would scratch my eyes out, if I did. You must go to the proper department."

I could not help watching the receding form of the President, as with long, indifferent strides he wended his way towards the Capitol. What a dreadful responsibility rested on .that man ! The hopes of millions of Republicans throughout the world were fixed upon him ; while twenty millions of his own people looked to him for the salvation of the Republic, and four millions of poor down-trodden slaves in the South looked to him for freedom.

Mr. Lincoln was no ordinary man. He had a quick and ready perception of facts, a retentive memory, and a logical turn of mind, which patiently and unwaveringly followed every link in the chain of thought on every subject which he investigated. He was honest, temperate, and forgiving. He was a good man—a man of noble and kindly heart. I never heard him speak unkindly of any man; even the rebels received no word of anger from him.

CONFEDERATES IN CANADA.

Immediately upon my arrival in Montreal, I sought opportunities to familiarize myself with the names, habits, and occupations of the various Confederates in Canada. I had but little difficulty in accomplishing this purpose, as the Confederates looked upon all Canadians as their friends.

The principal Confederate agent in Canada at that time, was an ex-Member of Buchanan's administration. The contemptible conduct of this man (while still a member of the Government), in warning the rebels of Charleston of the sailing of the Steamer " Star of the West," with provisions for the beseiged garrison at Fort Sumpter, will furnish a good index to his character.

The plots and schemes devised by him and his subordinates to furnish the rebels with clothing, boots and shoes, &c., *via* Nassau and Cuba, and to keep open a channel of communication with the Confederate States, kept me continually on the *qui vive* to frustrate their designs.

REBEL POSTAL SERVICE.

Toward the close of 1862, I received satisfactory information that a regular system of postal service was in operation between the Confederate States and Europe, *via* Canada. Diligently and earnestly I sought for a clue, week after week passed away, but nothing was discovered. I placed detectives on all the trains leaving Montreal, with instructions to closely watch every stranger, and especially those of southern aspect. All my efforts, however, were unsuccessful.

I finally concluded to go to Detroit, and institute some enquiries in that section. With that object in view, I sent for a cabman (one that I usually employed), to convey me to the depot for the 9 p. m. night train west; he came to inform me that it would be impossible for him to drive me that night, as he was obliged to take a lady from Lapraire to Champlain, a small village in the State of New York, not far from the boun-

dary line between Canada and the United States.
He said he had a brother living at Laprarie, who
was regularly employed to carry a lady once a
fortnight from Laprarie to Champlain ; but that
he was ill, and had sent for him to take his place.
Some further questions from me elicited the fact
that my cabman had on one former occasion
filled his brother's place to carry the same lady
over the same route.

My suspicions were now aroused, I felt confident that this lady had something to do with the
Confederate postal service, and I closely ques-
tioned him as to her appearance and habits, and
ostensible business, and why she travelled in
such an unusual manner and by such a round-
about route.   I put these questions in such a
way as not to excite suspicion in his mind as to
my object.   The information I obtained from
him was of such importance that I decided to
reach Champlain in advance of the cabman and
his strange passenger.   I consequently took the
evening train to Rouse's Point, and from thence
was driven in a carriage to Champlain.

I engaged quarters at the principal hotel in
the village, and in a short time won the
confidence of the talkative and consequential
little landlord, who finally, on my referring to

the lady in question, informed me that she was a Mrs. "Williams," (an *alias*, no doubt,) an agent for a religious tract society ; that she passed over this route from Canada about once a fort-night ; and that she was a very excellent person indeed. He, however, knew nothing about her, except that she said she was a tract distributer, travelling between Upper Canada and Boston. He finally remarked, "I expect her here either to-night or to-morrow night, on her way to Boston. She always arrives here in the night : sometimes it's early morning."

Securing a front bed-room, I was in a position to observe whoever came down the road leading from Canada, as the hotel fronted the road. Patiently I waited at the window from 10 p.m. to 3 a.m., looking out into the darkness. Shortly after three o'clock, I heard the rumbling of an approaching carriage coming down the road, and in a short time a cab drove up, and I saw my Montreal cabman alight and open the door of the carriage, from which a lady, closely muffled, stepped and entered the house. She was placed in a room on the opposite side of the hall to the one I occupied. To prevent her leaving the house without my knowledge, I determined to remain awake the rest of the night. At six o'clock I saw my cabman drive away towards Canada.

At the breakfast table, I sat *vis-a-vis* with the object of my search.   She was a keen, intelligent, witty, and handsome woman of medium size, with black eyes and hair, about 45 years of age. She conversed quite freely with the landlord's wife, but at times she would check herself, betraying a startled half-frightened look. Her conversation was principally upon her experiences as an agent of a "Religious Tract Society." At length an opportunity offered for me to engage in conversation with her.   When I informed her that I was Canadian, she became less reserved in her manner, and chatted familiarly on her trips through Canada. I soon learned that it was her intention to go to Rouse's Point by the noon train,

As soon as breakfast was over, I telegraphed to a detective at Rouse's Point to meet me, on the arrival of the train, prepared to make an arrest. When Mrs. Williams was seated in the car, I took a seat near her, to prevent her from escaping. Before the train reached the Point, it slackened up, and a detective officer came into the cars. I pointed out Mrs. Williams to him, and ordered him to take her to his house as soon as she stepped from the car, to watch every movement she made, and not permit her to have any communication with confederates.

ARREST OF A REBEL MAIL CARRIER.

As soon as the train entered the depot at Rouse's Point, the detective arrested her, and, with the aid of an assistant, took her to his house, where I immediately followed. I directed the wife of the detective to rigidly search her, and, if any documents were found, to call her husband and give them to him. Notwithstanding her protests, tears, and prayers, Mrs. Williams was thoroughly searched, and with good results, for eighty-two letters were found sewed into her under garments. The majority of them were addressed to rebel emissaries in Europe, the balance, to private individuals in the Northern States. After copying the address, and placing a number on each letter, I secured them safely on my person, and telegraphed to the President the substance of the above facts. In less than an hour I received instructions to hasten to Washington with the confiscated letters.

Before leaving Rouse's Point I had an interview with Mrs. Williams, during which I offered to secure her release, providing she would disclose certain information, that I knew she possessed, relative to the rebel mail route from the Confederacy to Europe *via* Canada. She, however, positively refused, and declared that

10

she would die in prison before she would disclose the secret.

Having instructed the officer to keep Mrs. Williams under close arrest until he received further orders from me, I left for Washington. On my arrival there (about midnight), I went direct to the Executive mansion, and sent my card to the President, who had retired to bed. In two or three minutes the porter returned, and requested me to accompany him to the President's office, where, in a short time, Mr. Lincoln would join me. The room into which I was ushered, was the same in which I had spent several hours with the President on the occasion of my first interview with him fourteen months before. Scattered about the floor, and lying open on the table, were several military maps and documents indicating recent use. On the wall I observed a picture of John Bright, of England.

INTERVIEW WITH PRESIDENT LINCOLN.

In a few minutes, the President came in, and received me in the most friendly manner. I expressed my regret at disturbing him at such an hour. He replied in a good humoured manner, saying, "No, no, you may route me up whenever you please. I have slept with

one eye open since I came to Washington ;
I never close both, except when an office-seeker
is looking for me."

" I am glad (referring to a letter I had sent
him) you are pleased with the Emancipation
Proclamation (issued a few weeks previously),
but there is work before us yet ; we must make
that Proclamation effective by victories over our
enemies. It's a paper bullet after all, and of no
account, except we can sustain it."

The President's efforts being now directed to
give freedom to the poor, despised, and long
suffering people of the South, I expressed my
belief that God would now aid the cause of the
Union. He replied, " Well, I hope so ! but the
suffering and misery that attends this conflict,
is killing me by inches. I wish it was over."

CONFISCATED REBEL DESPATCHES.

I then laid before the President the " rebel
mail." He carefully examined the address of
each letter, making occasional remarks. At
length he found one addressed to an ex-Presi-
dent of the United States, then residing in
New Hampshire, and another to an ex-Attorney
General of the United States, also a resident
of that State. He appeared much surprised,

and remarked with a sigh, but, without the
slightest tone of asperity, " I will have copies
made of these letters, after which they shall be
sent enclosed in official envelopes to these
parties." When he had finished examining the
addresses, he tied up all those addressed to
private individuals, saying, " I will not bother
with them ; but these look like official letters :
I guess I'll go through them now." He then
opened one after the other, and read their contents slowly and carefully.

While he was thus occupied, I had an excellent opportunity of studying this extraordinary
man. A marked change had taken place in his
countenance since my first interview with him.
He looked much older, and bore traces of
having passed through months of painful anxiety
and trouble. There was a sad, serious look in
his eyes that spoke louder than words of the
disappointments, trials, and discouragements he
had encountered since the war began. The
wrinkles about the eyes and forehead were
deeper ; the lips were firmer, but indicative of
kindness and forbearance. The great struggle
had brought out the hidden riches of his noble
nature, and developed virtues and capacities
which surprised his oldest and most intimate
friends. He was simple but astute : he pos-

sessed the rare faculty of seeing things just as they are : he was a just, charitable, and honest man.

REBELS IN NEW BRUNSWICK.

Having finished reading a letter, he said : " Read this (handing me a letter signed by the Confederate Secretary of State), and tell me what you think of it." The letter was addressed to the rebel envoy at the French Court, and stated that preparations were being made to invade the Eastern frontier of the United States in the vicinity of Calais, Maine. It also expressed. the opinion that an attack in so unexpected a quarter would dishearten the Northern people, and encourage the Democrats to oppose the continuation of the war.

I told the President that this confirmed the truth of the information I had received several weeks previously, and satisfied me that the rebels would make an attempt to raid on some of the Eastern States from the British Provinces. He replied : "I wish you would go to New Brunswick, and see what the rebels are up to. The information contained in these despatches is of great importance. Two of them I cannot read, as they are written in cipher ; but I'll find some way to get at their contents."

I then rose to go, saying that I would go to
the hotel, and have a rest. " No, no ! it is now
three o'clock ; you shall stay here while you
are in town.   Come with me, I'll find you a
bed," said the President ; and, leading the way,
he took me into a bedroom, saying : "Take a
good sleep, you shall not be disturbed." Bidding
me "Good-night," he left the room to go back
and pore over the rebel letters until daylight,
as he afterwards told me.

If ever the Almighty raised up an individual
to perform a special service, that person was
Abraham Lincoln.   No parent could evince a
greater interest in the welfare of his family than
he did for the safety and influence of his country.
Every faculty he possessed was devoted to the
salvation of the Union.

I did not awake from my sleep until eleven
o'clock in the forenoon, soon after which Mr.
Lincoln came to my room, and laughingly
said : "When you are ready, I'll pilot you down
to breakfast," which he did ; and, seating himself at the table, expressed his fears that trouble
was brewing in the Province of New Brunswick ;
that he had gathered further information on that
point from the correspondence, that convinced
him that such was the case.   He was here

interrupted by a servant, who handed him a card; upon reading which he left me, saying, "Come up to my room after breakfast."

On entering his room, I found him busily engaged in writing, at the same time repeating in a low voice the words of a poem, which I remembered reading many years before. When he stopped writing, I asked him who was the author of that poem. He replied, "I do not know. I have written the verses down from memory at the request of a lady who is much pleased with them. I wish I knew who was the author of them." He passed the sheet on which he had written the verses to me, saying, "Have you ever read them?" I replied that I had many years ago; and that I should be happy to have a copy of them in his handwriting, when he had time and inclination for such work. He said, "Well, you may keep that copy, if you wish."

The following is the poem as copied from Mr. Lincoln's manuscript given me on that occasion:

OH! WHY SHOULD THE SPIRIT OF MORTAL BE PROUD?

Oh! why should the spirit of mortal be proud?
Like a swift-fleeting meteor, a fast flying cloud,
A flash of the lightning, a break of the wave,
He passeth from life to his rest in the grave.

The leaves of the oak and the willows shall fade,
Be scattered around and together be laid ;
As the young and the old, the low and the high,
Shall crumble to dust, and together shall die.

The infant a mother attended and loved :
The mother that infant's affection who proved ;
The father, that mother and infant who blest—
Each, all are away to that dwelling of rest.

The maid, on whose brow, on whose cheek, in whose eye,
Shone beauty and pleasure—her triumphs are by ;
And alike from the minds of the living erased,
Are the memories of mortals that loved her and praised.

The hand of the king that the sceptre hath borne ;
The brow of the priest that the mitre hath worn ;
The eye of the sage, the heart of the brave,
Are hidden and lost in the depths of the grave.

The peasant, whose lot was to sow and to reap ;
The herdsman, who climbed with his goats up the steep ;
The beggar, who wandered in search of his bread,
Have faded away like the grass which we tread.

So the multitude goes, like the flower or the weed,
That withers away to let others succeed ;
So the multitude comes, even those we behold,
To repeat every tale that has often been told.

For we are the same our fathers have been ;
We see the same sights they often have seen ;
We drink the same stream, we see the same sun,
And run the same course our fathers have run.

The thoughts we are thinking, our fathers did think ;
From the death we are shrinking, our fathers did shrink ;
To the life we are clinging, our fathers did cling ;
But it speeds from us all like the bird on the wing.

They loved—but the story we cannot unfold ;
They scorned—but the heart of the haughty is cold ;
They grieved—but no wail from their slumbers will come.
They joyed—but the tongue of their gladness is dumb.

They died ; ah ! they died. We things that are now ;
That walk on the turf that lies over their brow,
And make in their dwelling a transient abode—
Meet the things that they met on their pilgrimage road.

Yea, hope and despondency, pleasure and pain,
Are mingled together in sunshine and rain ;
And the smile and the tear, and the song and the dirge,
Still follow each other like surge upon surge.

'Tis the wink of an eye, the draught of a breath,
From the blossom of health to the paleness of death,
From the gilded saloon to the bier and the shroud.
Oh ! why should the spirit of mortal be proud.

OFF TO NEW BRUNSWICK.

The rebel documents contained abundant evidence that the Confederate Government was organizing a band in Canada to raid upon the United States frontier, and the President requested me to "go to New Brunswick, and ascertain what the rebels were up to in that quarter."

That night I left Washington, and arrived in Boston in time to take the steamer for St. John, N. B. The boat was crowded with passengers ; and I had to share my stateroom with a gentleman who came aboard at Portland. The fea-

tures of my room companion were dark and
coarse ; his hair black and curling. He was
about six feet in height, of tough and wiry frame.
His language and general appearance was strikingly Southern. I retired to my berth before
him, selecting the top one, that I might the
more readily observe him ; for I had already
concluded that my room-companion was a
Confederate.

OCCUPY A ROOM WITH A REBEL.

When he entered the stateroom, he introduced himself as the owner of one of the
berths, and said : "I am glad you are not a
Yankee." I asked him how he knew that. He
replied : "I asked the clerk, and he said you
were a Canadian ; besides, you don't look like a
Yankee." "Well," I said, "you do not look like
a Canadian or a Yankee either ; I would take
you to be a Southern military officer." This
touched his vanity, and he admitted that he
had been in the military service of the Confederacy, but that he was now engaged on
special service. I felt now that I had sprung
the mine. I told him that I thought the Confederate Government were blind to their own
interests, in this, that no advantage had been
taken of the Canadian frontier to harass and
annoy the Yankees along the border.

WAR ON THE UNITED STATES FRONTIER.

"Well," said he, "we have had all we could do to keep the Yanks from our homes; but they will soon know how it feels to have the war carried into their own homes. I tell you, before long, you will hear something exciting." I replied: "I have heard that so frequently that I don't place much reliance upon such reports." I saw he was nettled at what I had said, and hoped it would make him indiscreet. He remained silent a moment, and then said: "What I have told you is the truth, and before two weeks are over you will hear something exciting from Eastport. I don't mind telling you, because you are a Canadian, and the Canadians are all on our side. Yes, sir; we have already a number of picked men in St. Andrews and St. Johns, New Brunswick, and we have a good supply of stores on Grand Menan Island. I expect thirty men from Canada next week. As soon as they arrive, we shall all go to Grand Menan, and prepare for an attack on Eastport; and, by —————, we intend to wipe it out. And then we shall attack Calais in the rear, and, if hard pressed, retreat into New Brunswick." This astounding news corroborated the information obtained from the captured letters.

ARREST OF A REBEL OFFICER.

On the arrival of the steamer at Eastport, I secured the arrest of my new acquaintance, and had him placed in prison. I telegraphed to Washington the information obtained from the rebel officer, and a gunboat was sent from Portland to Eastport. In forty-eight hours from my arrival, Eastport and Calais were fully prepared to meet the raiders. The Provincial authorities were also warned from Washington, and prompt steps taken to prevent any infraction of the Neutrality Laws on the New Brunswick border.

Returning to Portland, I sent the President a detailed narrative of the facts above related, and then returned to Montreal. In a few days, I received the following letter from Mr. Lincoln :—

EXECUTIVE MANSION,

Washington, Feb. 9, 1863.

MY DEAR SIR,—

I tender you my warmest thanks for the effective and invaluable services you have recently rendered me.   *   *   *   *   *

Accept my best wishes for your prosperity and happiness,

[*Fac-simile of signature.*]

PERSECUTION OF JOSHUA R. GIDDINGS.

The cruel and unnecessary arrest of the Hon.
Joshua R. Giddings, Consul General of the
United States, at Montreal, for the alleged con-
nivance at the kidnapping of one Redpath, was
incited by the Confederates in Montreal. Redpath had fled to Canada to escape punishment for
crimes committed during the draft riots in New
York. A detective officer was sent to Montreal
to arrest him. He was arrested, ironed, placed
in a close carriage, and driven to the depot.
Where he was then guarded by an assistant
while the New York detective went to the
United States Consulate, and told Mr. Giddings
that he had arrested a man charged with murder
in New York ; and that having complied with
the requirements of the Extradition Treaty,
he wished Mr. Giddings to give him a letter to
General Dix advising the General to compensate
the detective for the services of an assistant
required to convey Redpath to New York. Mr.
Giddings, without ascertaining (for which he was
in fault) whether all the formalities of the extradition treaty had been complied with, gave the
detective a note to General Dix, in which he
simply requested the General to remunerate the
detective for the service of an assistant

When the detective reached New York with his prisoner, Redpath obtained legal advice. The result of which was, that the Canadian authorities demanded the return of Redpath to Canada. He was consequently brought back and liberated. Then the Southern agents in Montreal, took charge of this criminal, and induced him to prosecute Mr. Giddings. This was done to gratify their feelings of hatred toward a man who had for thirty years fought for the cause of human freedom.

HIS ARREST.

Mr. Giddings was arrested on Sunday evening while dining at the house of a friend. The arrest was made on a day and at an hour when it was hoped he would be unable to obtain bail, and consequently would have to lay in jail over night. Messrs. Harrison Stephens and Ira Gould, two prominent and wealthy citizens of Montreal. gave bonds for *thirty thousand dollars* for Mr. Giddings's appearance at the trial of the case. Thus his enemies were baulked in their mean attempt to throw an innocent old man into prison. Mr. Giddings was in poor health at the time this outrage was perpetrated ; and he fretted and grieved over it continually. After the rebel agents had used Redpath for their purpose, they cast him off. I concluded it was now

a good time to get rid of Redpath and this persecution of Mr. Giddings.   I found the miserable
creature after considerable search, and prevailed
upon him to withdraw the suit, and confess that
he had been urged by the Confederate agents in
in Montreal to take action against Mr. Giddings.
This persecution, I have no doubt, hastened the
death of this noble old standard-bearer of liberty.

DEATH OF MR. GIDDINGS.

He died suddenly while amusing himself with
a game of billiards in the St. Lawrence Hall.
In Congress, Mr. Giddings stood shoulder to
shoulder with John Quincy Adams, in resist-
ing the tyrannical and despotic demands of
the slave drivers.   On one occasion when Mr.
Giddings was addressing the House in behalf of
freedom, a Southern member approached him
with a bowie knife in his hand, and threatened
to kill him on the spot, if he did not cease speaking.   Mr. Giddings was immediately surrounded
by his friends, and continued his speech, while
the cowardly ruffian who threatened him sneaked
back to his seat.   Mr. Giddings was not only a
good man, but he was morally and physically a
brave man.   He espoused the cause of the slave
at a time when an abolitionist was despised and
persecuted ; and he remained all his life a warm

and constant friend of the oppressed. The
many happy hours passed in his company, during the darkest periods of the war, will ever
remain bright spots in my memory.

STEPS TOWARD EMANCIPATION.

The following Acts and Proclamation indicate
the progressive steps by which, in the end, complete emancipation was reached.

Attention is hereby called to an Act of Congress, entitled
"An Act to make an additional article of war," approved
March 13, 1862, and which Act is in the words and figures
following :—

*Be it enacted by the Senate and House of Representatives of
the United States of America in Congress assembled:* That
hereafter the following shall be promulgated as an additional
article of war, for the government of the army of the United
States, and shall be obeyed and observed as such :

Article. All officers or persons in the military or naval service of the United States are prohibited from employing any
of the forces under their respective commands for the purpose
of returning fugitives from service or labor, who may have
escaped from any persons to whom such labor is claimed to be
due, and any officer who shall be found guilty by a court-mar-
tial of violating this article, shall be dismissed from the service.

SEC. 2. *And be it further enacted,* That this Act shall take
effect from and after its passage.

Also, to the ninth and tenth sections of an Act entitled,
"An Act to suppress insurrection, to punish treason and
rebellion, to seize and confiscate the property of rebels, and
for other purposes," approved July 17, 1862, and which
sections are in the words and figures following :—

SEC. 9. *And be it further enacted*, That all slaves or persons who shall hereafter be engaged in rebellion against the Government of the United States, or who shall in any way give aid or comfort thereto, escaping from such persons and taking refuge within the lines of the army ; and all slaves captured from such persons or deserted by them and coming under the control of the Government of the United States ; and all slaves of such persons found on (or being within) any place occupied by rebel forces and afterward occupied by the forces of the United States, shall be deemed captures of war, and shall be forever free of their servitude, and not again held as slaves.

SEC. 10. *And be it further enacted*, That no slave escaping into any State, territory, or the district of Columbia, from any of the States shall be delivered up, or in any way impeded or hindered of his liberty, except for crime or some offence against the laws, unless the person claiming said fugitive shall first make oath that the person to whom the labor or service of such fugitive is alleged to be due, is his lawful owner, and has not been in arms against the United States in the present rebellion, nor in any way given aid and comfort thereto ; and no person engaged in the military or naval service of the United States shall, under any pretence whatever, arsume to decide on the validity of the claim of any person to the service or labour of any other person, or surrender up any such person to the claimant, on pain of being dismissed from the service.

THE EMANCIPATION PROCLAMATION.

By the President of the United States of America.

Whereas, on the twenty-second day of September, in the year of our Lord one thousand eight hundred and sixty-two, a Proclamation was issued by the President of the United States, containing among other things the following, to wit :

"That on the first day of January, in the year of our Lord one thousand eight hundred and sixty-three, all persons held as slaves within any State, or designated part of a State, the people whereof shall then be in rebellion against the United States, shall be then, thenceforth and *forever free*, and the Executive Government of the United States, including the military and naval authorities thereof, will recognize and

11

maintain the freedom of such persons, and will do no act or acts to repress such persons, or any of them, in any efforts they make for their actual freedom.

"That the Executive will, on the first day of January aforesaid, by proclamation, designate the States and parts of States, if any, in which the people thereof respectively shall then be in rebellion against the United States, and the fact that any State or the people thereof, shall on that day be in good faith represented in the Congress of the United States by members chosen thereto at elections wherein a majority of the qualified voters of such State shall have participated, shall, in the absence of strong countervailing testimony, be deemed conclusive evidence that such State and the people thereof are not then in rebellion against the United States."

Now, therefore, I, ABRAHAM LINCOLN, President of the United States, by virtue of the power in me vested as Commander-in-Chief of the Army and Navy of the United States in time of actual armed Rebellion against the authority and government of the United States, and as a fit and necessary war measure for suppressing said Rebellion, do, on this first day of January, in the year of our Lord one thousand eight hundred and sixty-three, and in accordance with my purpose so to do, publicly proclaim for the full period of one hundred days from the day of the first above-mentioned order, and designate, as the States and part of States wherein the people thereof respectively are this day in rebellion against the United States, the following, to wit : ARKANSAS, TEXAS, LOUISIANA (except the Parishes of St. Bernard, Palquemines, Jefferson, St. John, St. Charles, St. James, Ascension, Assumption, Terre Bonne, Lafourche, St. Mary, St. Martin, and Orleans, including the City of Orleans), MISSISSIPPI, ALABAMA, FLORIDA, GEORGIA, SOUTH CAROLINA, NORTH CAROLINA, and VIRGINIA (except the forty-eight counties designated as West Virginia, and also the counties of Berkeley, Acconac, Northampton, Elizabeth City, York, Princess Ann, and Norfolk, including the cities of Norfolk and Portsmouth), and which excepted parts are, for the present, left precisely as if this Proclamation had not been issued.

And by virtue of the power and for the purpose aforesaid, I do order and declare that *all persons held as slaves* within said designated States and parts of States *are and henceforward* SHALL BE FREE ! and that the Executive Government

of the United states, including the Military and Naval authorities thereof, will recognize and maintain the freedom of said
persons.

And I hereby enjoin upon the people so declared to be free,
to abstain from all violence, unless in necessary self-defence,
and 1 recommend to them that in all cases, when allowed,
they labour faithfully for reasonable wages.

And I further declare and make known that such persons
of suitable condition will be received into the armed service
of the United States to garrison forts, positions, stations, and
other places, and to man vessels of all sorts in said service.

And upon this act, sincerely believed to be an act of
justice, warranted by the Constitution, upon military necessity, I invoke the considerate judgment of mankind and the
gracious favour of Almighty God.

In testimony whereof I have hereunto set my name, and
caused the seal of the United States to be affixed.

> Done at the City of Washington, this first day of
> January, in the year of our Lord one thousand
> [L. S.] eight hundred and sixty-three, and of the
> Independence of the United States the eighty-
> seventh.

ABRAHAM LINCOLN.

By the President.—WILLIAM H. SEWARD,
Secretary of State.

THE REPUBLICAN PLATFORM OF 1864 (LINCOLN AND JOHNSON).

The National Convention which assembled at Baltimore on
the 7th of June, 1864, and there nominated ABRAHAM LIN-
COLN for re-election as President, with ANDREW JOHNSON as
Vice-President, adopted and presented to the American people
the following :—

Resolved, That, as Slavery was the cause, and now consti-
tutes the strength, of this rebellion, and as it must be always
and everywhere hostile to the principles of Republican government, justice, and the national safety demand its utter and

complete extirpation from the soil of the Republic; and that
we uphold and maintain the acts and proclamations by which
the Government, in its own defence, has aimed a death-blow
at this gigantic evil.   We are in favour, furthermore, of such
an amendment to the Constitution, to be made by the people
in conformity with its provisions, as shall terminate and for
ever prohibit the existence of Slavery within the limits of the
jurisdiction of the United States.

PRESIDENT LINCOLN'S SECOND INAUGURAL ADDRESS, MARCH 4, 1865.

FELLOW-COUNTRYMEN : At this second appearing to take
the oath of the Presidential office, there is less occasion for an
extended address than there was at the first.   Then a statement, somewhat in detail, of a course to be pursued seemed
very fitting and proper.   Now, at the expiration of four years,
during which public declarations have been constantly called
forth on every point and phase of the great contest which
still absorbs the attention and engrosses the energies of the
nation, little that is new could be presented.

The progress of our arms, upon which all else chiefly
depends, is as well known to the public as to myself, and it
is, I trust, reasonably satisfactory and encouraging to all.
With high hope for the future, no prediction with regard to
it is ventured.

On the occasion corresponding to this, four years ago, all
thoughts were anxiously directed to an impending civil war.
All dreaded it; all sought to avoid it.   While the inaugural
address was being delivered from this place, devoted altogether
to saving the Union without war, insurgent agents were in
the city seeking to destroy it without war—seeking to dissolve
the Union and divide the effects by negotiation.   Both parties
deprecated war, but one of them would make war rather than
let the nation survive ; and the other would accept war rather
than let it perish, and the war came.

One-eighth of the whole population were coloured slaves,
not distributed generally over the Union, but localized in the
Southern part of it.   These slaves constituted a peculiar and
powerful interest.   All knew that this interest was somehow
the cause of the war.   To strengthen, perpetuate, and extend

this interest, was the object for which the insurgents would rend the Union even by war, while the Government claimed no right to do more than to restrict the territorial enlargement of it.

Neither party expected for the war the magnitude or the duration which it has already attained. Neither anticipated that the cause of the conflict might cease with, or even before the conflict itself should cease. Each looked for an easier triumph, and a result less fundamental and astounding.

Both read the same Bible, and pray to the same God; and each invokes the aid against the other. It may seem strange that any man should dare to ask a just God's assistance in wringing their bread from the sweat of other men's faces; but let us judge not, that we be not judged. The prayers of both could not be answered. That of neither has been answered fully. The Almighty has his own purposes. "Woe unto the world because of offences, for it must needs be that offences come; but woe to that man by whom the offence cometh." If we shall suppose that American slavery is one of these offences, which, in the providence of God, must needs come, but which, having continued through His appointed time, He now wills to remove, and that He gives to both North and South this terrible war as the woe due to those by whom the offence came, shall we discern therein any departure from those divine attributes which the believers in a living God always ascribe to him? Fondly do we hope, fervently do we pray, that this mighty scourge of war may soon pass away. Yet, if God wills that it continue until all the wealth piled by the bondman's two hundred and fifty years of unrequited toil shall be sunk, and until every drop of blood drawn with the lash, shall be paid with another drawn by the sword; as was said three thousand years ago, so still it must be said, "The judgments of the Lord are true and righteous altogether."

With malice toward none, with charity to all, with firmness in the right, as God gives us to see the right, let us strive on to finish the work we are in; to bind up the nation's wounds; to care for him who shall have borne the battle, and for his widow and his orphans; to do all which may achieve and cherish a just and a lasting peace among ourselves and with all nations.

The following amendment to the Constitution of the United States was ratified by vote of the Legislative Branches of the United States Government, February 1, 1865 :—

ARTICLE XIII.

Sec. 1. Neither Slavery nor involuntary servitude, except as a punishment for crime whereof the party shall have been duly convicted, shall exist within the United States, or any place subject during their jurisdiction.

Sec. 2. Congress shall have power to enforce this article by appropriate legislation.

CHAPTER VI.

EXTRACTS FROM LETTERS.

THE following extracts from a few of the letters received by me during the great rebellion, are published with a view to illustrate the varied hopes and fears that animated leading Abolitionists during the contest between freedom and slavery. *Fac-similes* of the autograph signatures of the writers are given.

FROM HORACE GREELEY.

OFFICE OF THE TRIBUNE,

New York, May 19th, 1863.

Since the outbreak of our terrible war, I have made it a rule to be rarely or ever away from our city for any distance. I should like very much to meet you and Mr. Giddings at Gerrit Smith's next week, but it is not possible for me. * * *

Yours faithfully,

Horace Greeley.

FROM SECRETARY SEWARD.

DEPARTMENT OF STATE,

Washington, June 4th, 1863.

I take this occasion to renew my thanks for your solicitous attention to the interests of this Government.   *   *   *   *   Your zeal merits the highest praise.

Yours, very respectfully,

FROM JOSHUA R. GIDDINGS.

Montreal, October 13th, 1863.

*   *   *   *   *   I fully agree with you, my dear friend, that any act, command, or enactment, violative of the eternal principles of right and liberty, are void ; that they have none of the essence or elements of law ; that they are the mere mandates of despots ; that it is not only right for you to disregard such mandates, but it

is your duty. There can be no law which in-
vades the rights of any innocent being to life,
liberty, and happiness.   *   *   *   *

Your friend,

Joshua R. Giddings

FROM GERRIT SMITH.

Peterboro', August 31, 1864.

*   *   *   *   *   I had strong fears from
the first that you would be baffled. We thank
you for your noble and benevolent purpose, and
accept the will for the deed. I believe the
Heavenly Father means that my country shall
live ; she has more to fear just now from Northern demagogues than from Southern rebels.

Your friend,

Gerrit Smith

FROM WENDELL PHILLIPS.

Boston, September 4th, 1864.

Mr. Lincoln may, probably does, wish the grand result, freedom to the negro but he is too much a *border statesman* in his opinions. Hence the negro is not to him a *man* in the full sense. Hence he overrates the prejudices and comfort of the slaveholders. Consequently, though he desires the result, he hesitates at the MEANS. Public opinion has bayonetted him up to his present position, and may yet save us through him, or rather in spite of him; but it is a very dangerous risk to run. SETTLEMENT is a more dangerous hour than war. Hence I oppose Lincoln's re-election; prominent republicans dread it. The leading Senator of New England said lately, "Lincoln's election would be destruction—McClellan's would be damnation;" so the leaders are making an effort to induce Lincoln to withdraw, and unite all earnest men on a better candidate. If we effect that, we are safe; if not, there is great danger that McClellan will be elected, then we should have to rely wholly upon the people to prevent his doing the harm he intends. I trust the people fully; but dread such a trial. The aim of all true men is either to replace Lincoln, or to array such a force against him as will oblige him to surround himself with a Cabinet of different wood.

The task we have to do, is a very great one. Davis made a rebellion : it was all he could do.) Lincoln, by tampering, delay, indecision, and long tenderness for slavery, has made a Confederacy—united, proud, with friends and military strength.

With great regard, and many thanks for all you have done for us,

Wendell Phillips

FROM GERRIT SMITH.

Peterboro', October 20th, 1864.

I am glad to learn that your heart is set on Lincoln's re-election. *   *   * This nation will live. It has given ample proof that it can withstand both foreign and domestic foes ; both Northern and Southern rebels. Yes, this nation will live to see herself and the whole continent free from oppressors—not from slaveholders only, but from Imperial despots also. As life is the law of righteousness, so death is the law of wickedness ; and the wickedness of the democratic party is nearing that extreme limit, where wickedness dies of itself. Be of good cheer—God is for us.

Your friend,

GERRIT SMITH.

FROM CHARLES SUMNER.

SENATE CHAMBER,

January 31st, 1865.

*   *   *   *   *   God bless your patriotic labor in our behalf. You have done a noble work, and deserve the thanks of every true American. Accept my best wishes and believe me.

Fathfully yours,

FROM GERRIT SMITH.

Peterboro', March 10th, 1865.

Many thanks for this excellent likeness of our dear friend Giddings. I hope to meet him in heaven. * * * *

The end of the terrible rebellion is at hand. I hope to hear this week of the capture of the remainder of Lee's army, and of the taking of Mobile. Heaven bless you for your active interest in our cause.

Your friend,

GERRIT SMITH.

FROM GEORGE B. LINCOLN.

Brooklyn, March 11th, 1865.

I thank you for your very able pamphlet that reached me yesterday. I am glad for your own section, that there is at least one (and I trust there are many) who will stand up for the liberty cause amidst so many who seem to owe the free people of the United States a grudge, and to give it exemplification in striking hands with the pirates and thieves who carry on the great rebellion. In the coming time no more mortifying chapter will be written in Canadian history, than the sad story of the aid and comfort given these enemies of mankind by her people. But I trust that the ancient philosophy will attain with you —that a few good men will save a city—so shall it be said, that for your fidelity and those who act with you, the wrong done us by the great mass of Canadian people, shall be forgotten. Slavery and rebellion which are two names for one thing nears its close. Thank God for the war ! Indeed, I have scarcely seen human hands in all this great struggle. His mighty arm has wielded the sword of justice, and in the North, as well as in the South, His wide swath can be tracked. The man who thought he was rich in money made out of southern trade, is to-day a *Pauper*. His children are Beggars—and the men who most of all, and singularly enough, took sides with the slaveholders in all political actions, were the Irish people, and they from their necessities, were found early, largely in the army. At least 50,000 of these people have gone out from us to return no more forever. A very great number are among us carrying an armless coat sleeve, or some other mark of rebel work. I hope to meet you in Canada the coming summer. Again, thanking you in behalf of our liberty-loving people for your good wishes.

Yours very truly,

GEO. B. LINCOLN.

FROM GOVERNOR FENTON.

EXECUTIVE DEPT., STATE OF NEW YORK.

Albany, April 11th, 1865.

* * * * I thank you in behalf of the loyal people of this State, for your patriotic services in our behalf. Your interest in our cause, I assure you, is highly appreciated.

Again, thanking you,

I remain yours respectfully.

R. E. FENTON.

———

FROM WILLIAM LLOYD GARRISON.

Boston, May 13, 1865.

* * * * * Your active and sympathetic interest, in behalf of the freedmen of our country, will do much to engender kindly feelings between the United States and Canada. * * * *

Yours, for universal freedom,

Wm. Lloyd Garrison.

FROM JOHN GREENLEAF WHITTIER (THE
QUAKER POET).

Amesburg, 27, 5th mo., 1865.

MY DEAR FRIEND,

It gives me great satisfaction to see
the friends of freedom in Canada and England
acting in behalf of the freedmen of the United
States. * * *

The tears which both nations are shedding
over the grave of our beloved President are
washing out all the bitter memories of miscon-
ception and estrangement between them. So
good comes of the evil.

> Oh, Englishmen! in hope and creed,
>   In blood and tongue our brothers;
> We too are heirs of Runymede,—
> And Shakespeare's fame and Cromwell's deed
>   Are not alone our mother's.
>
> Thicker than water in one rill,
>   Through centuries of story;
> Our Saxon blood has flow'd, and still—
> We share with you the good and ill,
>   The shadow and the glory.

Thine truly,

FROM WILLIAM CULLEN BRYANT.

Roslyn, Long Island,

June, 3rd, 1865.

*   *   *   *   I am glad to know the cause of the United States has so strenuous a defender in Canada.   Your zealous and patriotic labours merit the thanks of all who desire the prosperity of this country.   *   *

Faithfully yours,

W. C. Bryant

———

FROM WENDELL PHILLIPS.

Boston, June 12th, 1865.

I will mail you, with this, my last two speeches and evening talks on Lincoln's death, from which you will get a fuller view of my present position than I could give you in a note.

I will only add, that since those speeches, I have become more and more anxious and doubtful about the policy our President will pursue. The Cabinet are about equally divided on the question of negro suffrage. But we hope to make an active use of the interval before the next session of Congress, to manifest (I say

12

manifest, because it already exists,) such a determined public opinion as will awe the Government into following that radical course in which
the masses are abundantly ready to support them.
Time will show what we can do.   Politicians are
slippery reliance in war times as well as in peace.
Thank you for all your active and zealous
efforts in our behalf.

Your friend,

Wendell Phillips

FROM GERRIT SMITH.

Peterboro', July 1st, 1865.

*   *   *   *   * Slavery has received its
death blow ; but it is by no means certain that
our nation will be saved or still united. We may
have first to pass through a war of races.   I am
not satisfied with the course our goverment is
pursuing in the matter of " reconstruction." My
poor, guilty country cannot be saved so long as it
hates and persecutes the black man. Our nation
is lost, if the Freedmen are denied the ballot.

Your friend,

Gerrit Smith

FROM GENERAL GARIBALDI.

Brescia (Italy), September, 1865.

* * * * I rejoice with you over the destruction of slavery in the American Republic. * * * * Cloisters and prisons are not His work. God made liberty—man made slavery.

Ever yours,

G. Garibaldi

———

FROM VICTOR HUGO.

HAUTEVILLE HOUSE,

August 13, 1865.

* • * * Freedom makes Light and Life. Slavery makes deafness in the soul.

Accept, sir, the homage of my respect.

Victor Hugo

CHAPTER VII.

EFFORTS TO AROUSE SYMPATHY FOR THE NORTH—LETTERS AND PAMPHLETS.

HE following letters and pamphlets I had published and circulated extensively throughout Canada, with a view to aid the cause of the North, by arousing sympathy, awakening humane and liberal sensibilities, and drawing more enlightened attention to the objects of the great struggle between freedom and slavery in the United States.

I felt persuaded that once the Canadian people were rightly informed as to the nature and objects of the slaveholders, their sympathies would be given to the North in her efforts to crush the rebellion, and prevent the establishment on this continent of a government

"With one great bloodstone for its mighty base."

" THE PRESENT WAR IS SIMPLY A CONFLICT BETWEEN SLAVERY
AND FREEDOM."—*Hon. Charles Sumner.*

THE SLAVEHOLDERS' REBELLION.

ITS INTERNAL CAUSES.

Every step in progress the world has made
since the advent of Christ, has been made from
the cross to the scaffold, and from stake to stake.
All the great truths relating to society and self-
government, have been first heard in the solemn
protests of dying martyrs and patriots, who have
yielded up their lives a sacrifice to obtain freedom and liberty for mankind.

The great contest now being waged in the
United States, is a struggle between a higher and
lower civilization—a continuation of the struggle
between light, liberty, and freedom, and the
ruling powers of wickedness and tyranny, which
began at the advent of our Saviour, and has
been continued by his apostles, and by martyrs
and patriots from that time to the present day.

Never, since the revolt of Satan against the
government of Jehovah, has there been a rebellion so utterly causeless and unjustifiable as the
Slaveholders' Rebellion. Actuated by the same
wicked ambition that moved Satan to rebel

against righteousness, peace, and justice in heaven, the slaveholders are seeking to overthrow the only really republican government on earth, and to erect upon its ruins a despotism of the vilest description—the foundation of which is to be human slavery ; and thus crush out forever the refuge and hope of liberty-loving men of every nation and people.

The rebellious slaveholders never furnished any list of grievances, never cited any acts of despotism on the part of the government against which they rebelled. Their only excuse was, that a party had come into power, the leaders of which had some moral feeling in reference to slavery. It could not be truthfully alleged that Mr. Lincoln proposed to infringe upon their state rights or peculiar privileges. No ; the actual and only object was (in case they proved successful in their appeal to arms), to found a slave empire upon this continent, and extend the baneful curse of slavery all over this land, from the Atlantic to the Pacific, and repudiate the God-given right to all men of life, liberty, and the pursuit of happiness. They wish to establish a government for the rich and powerful, that they may the more firmly rivet the chains of bondage and despotism upon the poor black people of this continent.

The slaveholders, and their supporters in the North, had for fifty years controlled the government of the United States, and used their patronage and power to advance the interests of slavery, and force compromise after compromise from the northern people. During the past eight years the Republican or anti-slavery party in the Free States had gained strength rapidly. Their principles were inimical to slavery, and especially to its extension to the great territories of the west. No attempt, however, was made or could be made constitutionally to interfere with slavery in those States where it was legalized by local enactments. Under the Federal Constitution, every State has the right to make such laws and enactments as will not conflict with the Constitution of the United States. The President has no power, in time of peace, to interfere with the institutions of any State, and there is clearly no such power in Congress. But, for thirty years the slaveholders had been seeking a pretext to rebel, and when the people of the Free States nominated as their candidate for the office of President, Abraham Lincoln, they at once declared that in case he was elected, they would never submit to the will of the majority, but would rebel and disrupt the nation, and establish a Confederacy, the corner stone of which should be human slavery.

For thirty years the gulf between the Free and Slave States had grown wider and wider. The conflict between freedom and slavery had become fiercer and more bitter year after year. The anti-slavery party, of which John Quincy Adams, Joshua R. Giddings, Gerrit Smith, and other noble advocates of freedom, were the founders, had increased and become a great, influential, and powerful party, spreading its influence and principles throughout the country. For many years after the inception of this party, its leaders and advocates were subjected to the most persistent abuse and persecution at the hands of slaveholders and their sympathisers in the North. But the little cloud that appeared no larger than a man's hand thirty years ago, now overshadows the whole Union.

The triumphant election of Abraham Lincoln, convinced the Southern despots that hereafter the power and influence of the General Government would be exerted to extend the blessings of freedom and liberty, and establish for ever the immortal principle that all men have "the inalienable right to life, liberty, and the pursuit of happiness."

True to their wicked purpose, the slaveholders precipitated the country into a bloody and cruel war, which has continued, with varied success, for nearly four years. I believe that out of this conflict will arise great good to mankind, and that, when this conflict is ended, freedom will be universal throughout the great American Republic. What a glorious future awaits the United States, when slavery is forever crushed, and the energies of her enlightened millions shall be devoted to extending the principles of freedom and self-government over the continent of America, and in welcoming the poor down-trodden masses of Europe!

The United States deserve the sympathy of every Christian man and nation, because they have espoused the cause of freedom, and are contending for the rights of man. And although the loss of life and suffering consequent upon the great struggle is to be deplored, I feel convinced it is all for the best; for had the North been successful in crushing the rebellion at an earlier period we would not have attained that result which every good man should desire—the abolition of human slavery.

With what gigantic strides the cause of freedom has advanced since the war broke out, and what glorious results have been worked out! At the outbreak of the rebellion,

there were four millions of human beings in
bondage in the Southern States, and the day of
deliverance seemed very remote. They were
held down by the most wicked, vile, and cruel
system of slavery ever devised ; and possessed
no right which a white man was bound to respect.

How different their condition at present!
Hundreds of thousands are now enjoying the
blessings of freedom and liberty, and the whole
power and influence of the Northern States is
being exerted in their behalf. The constitutional
amendment abolishing slavery throughout the
Union has passed both the Senate and House
of Representatives, and will shortly be ratified
by the required number of States to make it
an accomplished fact. When that glorious deed
is done, what an enviable and proud position
will the United States occupy! Cleansed from
the foul blot of slavery, it will be a beacon-
light to every people and nation. Several of
the former Slaveholding States have already
emancipated their slaves, and commenced
a new and glorious career in the new nation of
Free States. Thus the good work of emancipation goes on, and will continue until freedom is
universal.

THE RIGHTS OF MAN.

Our Almighty Father has given to all men the right to live, the right to enjoy the light of the sun, the right to breathe the vital air, to unfold his moral nature, to learn the laws that control his moral and physical being, to bring himself into harmony with these laws, and to enjoy that happiness which is consequent upon such obedience ; and wherever a human soul exists, that law applies. I mean by the term *soul* that immortal principle in man which exists hereafter ; and where such a soul exists there is the right to live, to attain knowledge, the right to sustain life, obey the laws of his Creator, and enjoy heaven and happiness, and the poorest slave on earth has this inalienable right ; and whoever deprives him of that right outrages both the laws of God and nature. In defiance of these sacred laws, four millions of innocent human beings have long been deprived of all these rights and subjected to a cruel bondage by the slaveholders of the South. Thank God, the hour of their deliverance is at hand ; and how severe the punishment now being meted out, by a just God, to those wicked and misguided men who sought to establish a government in violation of God's most sacred laws !

May 16th, 1865.

IN Memory of JOSHUA R. GIDDINGS, who died
May 27th, 1864, at Montreal.

Mr. Giddings was one of the truest, most con-
sistent, and courageous advocates of freedom in
the Northern States. For thirty years he faithfully laboured, both in and out of Congress, to
bring about the abolition of slavery, and before
he was called away from earth he was permitted to see the dawning of brighter and better
days for his country. Only one day prior to his
death he remarked to the writer, while conversing upon national topics, " I have but one desire
to live longer, and that is, to see the complete
triumph of the cause to which I have given
the energies of my life." This noble and venerable patriot was one of the few statesmen in
the Northern States who felt the humiliation
of sharing the responsibility of slavery.

The writer was honoured with the confidence
and regard of Mr. Giddings, and was with him
much during the last weeks of his life. He
possessed a kind and genial nature, and when
conversing upon the glory that he believed
awaited his country, when every human being
whether black or white, should be in possession
of the God-given right of freedom and equality,
his countenance would glow with animation and
joy.

Mr. Giddings was a thorough abolitionist in principle. He did not, like many of the statesmen of the present day, stop merely at emancipation, but demanded that every innocent man was entitled not only to liberty and equality before the law, but also to the right of suffrage. Thirty years ago he bravely advocated the cause of the poor down-trodden slave, when to be called an abolitionist was considered a disgrace and a dishonour ; neither threats of personal violence nor abuse could daunt the spirit of this heroic and Christian man ; and, from his first entrance into public life to the day of his decease, he never allowed an opportunity to escape him of advocating the cause of those in bondage. The poor slave always had in him a warm defender and true friend. His position on this great question, classes him with Wilberforce and Clarkson, names dear to humanity, who were the first in England to speak for the enslaved race. He strove with all his power to eradicate the foul blot of slavery from his native land ; and, before he took his departure for his heavenly home, he was permitted to catch a glimpse of the bright future in store for his country.

Few names will rank above his when the long conflict with slavery is ended, and justice done to those who fought for the right.

> " Angelic peace ! O stay not long,
> But sit beside the patriot's tomb,
> And sing an everlasting song,
> Of Freedom's triumph, Slavery's doom ;
> Unite the several links again,
> The golden links of every State,
> That men may tell their fellow men.
> Columbia stands, free, blest, and great."

June, 1865.

SLAVERY IN THE SOUTHERN STATES.

Human slavery has been denounced by all the great and good men of the Christian world, as a "relic of barbarism." The fathers of the American Republic, pronounced it an outrage, and deplored its existence ; and the Bible also rises up in judgment against this iniquitous institution.

Notwithstanding all this array of evidence against human slavery, the bold attempt has recently been made in this city, Toronto, by a pro-slavery clergyman, to inculcate the falsehood that human slavery was devised by our Heavenly Father, and is, consequently, in perfect accordance with His Almighty designs.

To the humane and enlightened among us, it may appear a work of supererogation to publicly

protest against this absurd pretension ; but I
deem it my duty, as an anti-slavery man, and in
presenting my protest, I shall avail myself of
the opportunity afforded me, of recording the
testimony of Washington, Jefferson, Madison,
Monroe, Patrick Henry, and John Randolph,—
all residents of Virginia, and the most illustrious
men of their day ; and thus show those in
Canada who sympathize with the slaveholders'
rebellion, the hideous serpent they are helping
to warm into life ; for the Vice-President of the
rebellious States, has declared that *" Slavery is
the chief Corner-stone of the Confederate Government."*

Is it possible, after reading the opinions of the
great and good men above quoted, and the testimony of the Bible, that any man, professing to
be a follower and believer in the meek and lowly
Jesus, can give his sympathies or countenance to
such a heaven-defying scheme ? Is it possible
that any liberty-loving Briton can countenance
the establishment of a government with such a
foundation, after reading the declaration of
Brougham and Wesley upon the vile and wicked
institution of slavery ? These great men knew
whereof they affirmed : they were familiar with
the laws of the Slave States, which are alone
sufficient to inspire horror in every human heart
or reflecting mind.

GEORGE WASHINGTON says : " There is not a man living who wishes more sincerely than I do to see a plan adopted for the abolition of slavery." *George Washington*, April 12th, 1786. "The scheme, my dear Marquis, which you propose as a precedent to encourage the emancipation of the black people in this country, from the state of bondage in which they are held, is a striking evidence of the benevolence of your heart."— *Washington to Layfette*, 1783.

" It is the most earnest wish of America to see an entire stop put to the *wicked* and *cruel* trade in slaves."—*Meeting at Fairfax, Va.*, presided over by Washington, July 18, 1784.

THOMAS JEFFERSON says, in his " *Notes on Slavery in Virginia* :" " I tremble for my country, when I reflect that God is just. His justness cannot sleep for ever."

JAMES MADISON says: "We have seen the mere distinction of colour, made in the most enlightened period of time, a ground of the most *oppresssive dominion* ever exercised by man over man."

JAMES MONROE says : "We have found that this evil has preyed upon the very vitals of the Union, and has been prejudicial to all the States in which it has existed."

JOHN RANDOLPH, of Roanoke, says, "I envy neither the head nor the heart of that man who defends slavery upon principle."

THOMAS JEFFERSON says: "One *day* of American slavery is worse than a *thousand years* of that which the American colonists arose in arms to oppose." Alluding to slave insurrections, he said: "The Almighty has no attribute that can take sides with us, in a contest with our slaves."

PATRICK HENRY says : "Slavery is *detestable.* We feel its fatal effects. We *deplore it with all the pity of humanity.*"

Surely here is evidence sufficient to convince any but the most prejudiced, of the iniquity of slavery as it exists in the South. The great men above quoted, were residents of Virginia, and the founders of the Republic.

LORD BROUGHAM says : "Tell me not of rights. Talk not of the property of the planter in his slaves. I deny the rights—I acknowledge not the property. The principles—the feelings of our common nature—rise in rebellion against it. Be the appeal made to the understanding or to the heart, the sentence is the same that rejects it. In vain you may tell me of laws that sanc-

18

tion such a claim.   There is a law above all the
enactments of human codes : it is the law written by the finger of God upon the heart of man,
and by that law, unchangeable and eternal, while
men despise fraud, and loathe rapine and abhor
blood, they shall reject with indignation the wild
and guilty fantasy that man can hold property
in man."

JOHN WESLEY declares, "slavery to be the
sum of all villainies."

MISS SARAH M. GRIMKE, daughter of the late
Judge Grimke, of the Supreme Court of South
Carolina, testifies as follows : " As I left my native land on account of slavery, and deserted the
home of my father to escape the sound, of the
lash and the shrieks of tortured victims, I would
gladly bury in oblivion the recollection of those
scenes with which I have been familiar.   But
that cannot be, they come over my memory like
goary spectres, and implore me with resistless
force, in the name of a God of mercy, in the
name of a crucified Saviour, for the sake of the
poor slave, to bear witness to the horrors of the
Southern prison-house."

Among the horrible barbarities she enumer-
ates, is the case of a young girl, thirteen years

old, who was flogged to death by her master.
She says : " I asked a prominent lawyer who
belonged to one of the first families in the State,
whether the murderer of this helpless child could
not be indicted ? and he cooly replied, " the slave
was Mr. ——'s property, and if he chose to suffer
the loss, no one else had anything to do with it."
She proceeds to say : " I felt there could be no
rest for me in the midst of such outrages and
pollutions."

THE BIBLE says :

" Remember them that are in bonds, as bound
with them."—*Heb.* xiii. 3.

" Hide the outcasts. Betray not him that
wandereth. Let my outcasts dwell with thee.
Be thou a covert to them from the face of the
spoiler."—*Isa.* xvi. 3, 4.

" Thou shalt not deliver unto his master the
servant which has escaped from his master unto
thee. He shall dwell with thee. Thou shalt not
oppress him."—*Deut.* xxiii. 15, 16.

"Whatsoever ye would that men should do
to you, do ye even so to them."—*Matt.* vii. 12.

" Is not this the fast I have chosen to loose the
bonds of wickedness, to undo the heavy burdens

and to let the oppressed go free, and that ye break every yoke ?"—*Isa.* lviii. 6.

" They have given a boy for an harlot, and sold a girl for wine, that they may drink."—*Joel* iii. 3.

" He that oppresseth the poor, reproacheth his Maker."—*Prov.* xiv. 31.

" Rob not the poor because he is poor ; neither oppress the oppressed.   For the Lord will plead their cause, and spoil the soul of them that spoil them."—*Prov.* xxii. 22, 23.

" Masters give unto your servants that which is just and equal ; knowing that ye also have a Master in heaven."—*Col.* iv. 1.

" Neither be ye called masters, for one is your Master, even Christ, and all ye are brethren."— *Matt.* xxiii. 8, 9.

" Woe unto him that useth his neighbour's service without wages, and giveth him not for his work."—*Jer.* xxii. 13.

" Behold, the hire of your labourers who have reaped down your fields, which is of you kept back by fraud, crieth ; and the cries of them which have reaped are entered into the ears of the Lord of Sabaoth.   Ye have lived in pleasure on the earth, and been wanton : ye have nour-

ished your hearts as in a day of slaughter."—
Jas. v. 4, 5.

The above quotations, from both the Old and
New Testaments, prove conclusively that the pre-
sumptuous assertion, that "slavery is sanctioned
by the Bible," has no foundation in fact. The
human heart, reason, religion, and, above all, the
Bible, rise up in judgment against it.

The universal law in the Slave States is, that
"the child follows the condition of the mother."
This is an index to many things. Marriage between white and coloured people, is forbidden
by law; yet a very large number of the slaves
are brown or yellow. How could this be, unless
their fathers or grandfathers had been white
men? But as their mothers were slaves, slave
laws pronounce them slaves also, subject to be
sold on the auction block, whenever the necessities or convenience of their masters and mis-
tresses require it, The sale of one's own children
has an ugly aspect *to those unaccustomed to it.*

Throughout the Slave States, no coloured
person's testimony can be taken against a white
man. Any drunken master or overseer may go
into the negro cabin, and commit any outrage
he pleases with perfect impunity, if no white
person is present who will witness against him.

Slave laws declare that "a slave is a chattel to all intents and purposes whatsoever." This involves the right to sell his wife and children, as if they were cattle. There are large numbers of fugitives from slavery in Canada, with many of whom I have conversed. I have seen the scars of the whip and branding iron, and have listened to their heart-broken sobs as they told of their wives and children torn from their arms to be sold.

Viewing slavery in the light of the above testimony, is there a Christian man in Canada who does not feel it an outrage upon his feelings to have it boldly and plausibly asserted that the Bible upholds such a heaven-defying pretension, that tramples upon the most sacred relations, making wife and child the wretched prey of lust and avarice ?

> *   *   *   "O execrable son ! so to aspire
> Above his brethren, to himself *assuming*
> Authority usurped, from God not given !
> He gave us only over beast, fish, fowl,
> Dominion absolute ; that right we hold
> By His donation ; but man over men
> He made not Lord, such title to Himself
> Reserving, human left from human free."
>   *Milton's Paradise Lost*, Bk. XII. 64, 73.

February 3, 1865.

REMARKS AT THE ANNUAL MEETING OF
THE "SOCIETY FOR THE ABOLITION OF
HUMAN SLAVERY," HELD IN MONTREAL,
OCTOBER 21ST, 1863.

LADIES AND GENTLEMEN,—My views upon
the subject of slavery are by many considered
ultra; but I have been an eye-witness to the
cruelty, injustice, and barbarity of that vile and
atrocious institution, and know whereof I speak.
In October, 1859, while on a visit to Richmond, Virginia, I was forcibly reminded of the
truth of the saying, "The wicked fleeth when no
man pursueth." I found the population of that
city in a condition of great excitement; a feeling
of dread and insecurity prevailed which extended
to every part of the State. You will naturally
ask the cause of this excitement, this feeling of
insecurity and dread. The people of Virginia
were at that time living under the protection of
a government intensely pro-slavery; they were
in the enjoyment of all their State rights: the
cause of this dread and insecurity in the minds
of slaveholders was produced by the sudden
darting of a ray of light from Harper's Ferry,—
a ray of light that penetrated the pending gloom
and ignorance which hung like a cloud over the
darkened minds of 4,000,000 enslaved human

beings. John Brown had stricken a blow on the confines of slavery, the echoes of which resounded on every plantation, and entered the humble cabin of the poor slave as well as the mansion of the proud and haughty slaveholder, and roused the long-deferred hope in the bosom of millions of poor, downtrodden, and long-suffering slaves that the hour of their deliverance from a cruel tyranny was at hand ; and prayers ascended from a thousand rude cabins to the Almighty Father for freedom, justice, and liberty. Is it a matter of surprise that a feeling of dread and insecurity was felt in the mansion of the proud and haughty master, when a million earnest prayers were going up to the throne of God for justice and freedom ?

It is not unusual to hear the tales of cruelty and oppression toward this unfortunate people spoken of as a fiction; and that interesting work of Mrs. Stowe (Uncle Tom's Cabin) has been declared by slaveholders and Northern sympathisers with slavery, as entirely imaginary and unworthy of belief.

Mr. President, I have read that and other kindred works upon the institution of slavery, and assure you I have witnessed scenes of oppression, cruelty, and brutality towards that inoffensive people in the Slave States, far exceeding anything described in works of the kind mentioned.

Slavery is demoralizing in its tendencies to the white as well as to the black, to the master as well as to the slave. Where it exists, it brutalizes and renders the white domineering, despotic and brutal. The black race is kept in a condition of the grossest ignorance, and the circulation of knowledge is guarded with a jealous eye, with a view to prevent the slave from gaining information. The discussion of subjects which would be likely to reach the darkened but alert mind of the coloured people, is sternly prohibited. For fifty years past, the Government of the United States has been under the control of Southern men, and they have persistently endeavoured to extend their domineering tyranny over the entire North; and until within the past twenty-five years, there were few prominent men in the North with sufficient moral courage to face the proud and overbearing dictation of the slave lords in the Senate and Congress. The venerable John Quincy Adams, and that noble veteran and apostle of freedom, the late Joshua R. Giddings took a firm and decided stand twenty-five years ago for freedom, and bravely asserted that all

men, black and white, had the "inalienable right
to life, liberty, and the pursuit of happiness;"
and for many years these two noble men with-
stood a united Senate and House of Congress,
and the cowardly and assassinlike threats and
abuse of the slave-drivers of the South. The
lamp lighted by Garrison, Adams, and Giddings,
continued to burn with increased brilliancy year
after year, and in many of the free States
societies were formed to promote the abolition
of Slavery by the dissemination of information
throughout the North, describing the actual condition of the poor downtrodden slaves and to
awaken an interest in behalf of that oppressed
people. The leaders in this movement had to
withstand the most vindictive persecution at
the hands of Southern men and their sympathisers in the North. Prominent upon the roll
of men who have rendered their names immortal
by the advocacy of the rights of man may be
mentioned the names of John Quincy Adams,
Joshua R. Giddings, William Lloyd Garrison,
Wendell Phillips, Gerritt Smith, Horace Greeley,
Charles Sumner, and other noble men and
women who have laboured with great zeal
and sacrifice to bring about the abolition of
human slavery in the United States. The
slaveholders used every influence in their power
to prevent discussions upon the subject of

slavery, and when they failed to meet the arguments of the anti-slavery men, they assumed the domineering and despotic attitude of the slave-driver, and attempted, by acts of cowardly brutality, to stifle discussion with the bowie-knife, pistol, and bludgeon. The late Mr. Giddings, when a member of Congress, and while addressing the House upon the rights of man, was threatened with instant death if he uttered another word upon the subject; but the brave old statesman well knew the cowardly character of slaveholders, and continued his address in defiance of the cowardly threat. And more recently the Hon. Charles Sumner was attacked while seated at his desk in the Senate Chamber, and nearly assassinated by a Southern member of Congress, while another Southerner stood over the victim of this brutal outrage with a cocked pistol, to prevent the bystanders from rendering aid to Mr. Sumner while his Southern *confrere*, with murderous intent, brutally assaulted an unarmed man. This outrage upon Mr. Sumner was committed because his arguments, proving the " Barbarism of Slavery," were unanswerable. In this manner the South has endeavoured to control the nation and extend and perpetuate the blighting curse of slavery. And when the slaveholders found they could no longer browbeat and force the liberty-loving people of the

North into acquiescence with their barbarous designs, they rebelled, and are now endeavoring to establish a government with slavery for its chief corner-stone. An eminent English statesman has asserted, in reference to the war in the United States, that "the North is fighting for empire, and the South for independence." This is a fallacy—the great struggle now being waged in the United States, is a continuance of the contest between freedom and slavery, that began thirty-five years ago in Congress ; and, thank God, the indications are, that slavery will go down beneath the blows of the freemen of the North.

It is unnecessary for me to occupy your attention any longer to convince you of the barbarity and demoralizing influence of slavery. Most of you have doubtless seen the photographs of the slave children from New Orleans ; the mother of these two innocent children was a slave, and the children of a slave mother follow her condition,—and these innocent children, as white as any child in Montreal, were destined for the slave market. This is not by any means an isolated case, but of frequent and daily occurrence in the Slave States. What do you think of a father selling his own child, and that child a pure innocent girl, as white, if not whiter than himself, and for the basest, vilest, and most loathsome purpose imaginable ? Thank God for the war ; may it continue until we no longer hear the sighs and groans of an oppressed and cruelly outraged people ! I believe the great principle of human freedom involved in this contest will ultimately triumph ; it may be the purpose of a just God to punish still more the people of the North, because of their complicity with the South in binding the chains of slavery upon the coloured people. But out of this great contest will arise the august form of Liberty demanding that all men—black and white—shall have an equal right to " Life, liberty, and the pursuit of happiness."

It is the custom in this country, and in England, to find fault with the President of the United States, because he has not done more towards liberating the slaves, and especially, because he failed to declare every slave in the Union free, when he issued the emancipation proclamation. I believe Mr. Lincoln has done all he could do constitutionally toward emancipation, and has kept pace with the public opinion of the country ; he may appear slow and over-cautious at times, but he has done what he has, after grave deliberation and much thought and

anxiety.   In issuing his emancipation proclamation, he acted in his capacity of Commander-in-
Chief of the Army of the United States ; he had
no power to interfere with the local institutions
of a State like Kentucky, not in actual rebellion.
I find from public documents that over one
million of slaves have been liberated, during
the past two years, and the good work goes
bravely on.   President Lincoln, in my estimation, merits the approbation and prayers of
every Christian man, for his efforts to crush
slavery ; and that God will help him and sustain
him, should be the earnest prayer of every true
lover of freedom.

AMERICAN RECONSTRUCTION.

The question of Reconstruction, which at
present is deeply agitating the public mind in
the United States, is one which almost equally
concerns all mankind as much as the American
people.   That the fruits of the great conquest
won by the North may not be entirely lost, is a
wish that is shared alike by the people of every
enlightened nation.

The policy of Reconstruction, now being pursued by President Johnson, is fraught with much danger to the permanent peace and welfare of the United States, and to the progress of Liberal principles throughout the world. The President's system of appointing, as Provisional Governors of the rebel States, men who have just returned from the ranks of the rebel army, and the indiscriminate pardoning and restoring to political rights of men who were prominent in their efforts to destroy the Government—the placing into political power of men who, by their infamous treachery, forfeited everything, even their lives, will, it is believed, work great and lasting injury to the cause of freedom in the Southern States.

Mr. Johnson maintains that the rebel acts of secession were null and void—that the rebel States have never been out of the Union—that the Federal authority was only temporarily obstructed by insurrection—that all acts done and laws enacted by rebel authority were illegal assumptions of power, and that all the people of the lately rebel States are required to do, to enable them to assume the rights and privileges they forfeited by their participation in rebellion, is to obtain pardon and take the oath of fidelity to the Federal Government, which they have, for four years been endeavouring to destroy;

and having conformed to the above requirements, they (the rebels) are to be reinstated to
all the rights, civil and political, of loyal citizens.
This is the policy adopted by the President,
and which, if persisted in, will deprive the loyal
people of the Union of the fruits of the great
victories they have nobly won by the sacrifice of
so much life and treasure.

The most recent information from the South
conveys the surprising intelligence that President Johnson has authorized the Provisional
Governors of Mississippi and South Carolina to
arm and organize a company of militia in each
county of these States; and as the whole white
population of both these States were rebels,
without exception, the militia, of course, will be
rebels, and zealous in their efforts to keep the
nominally free coloured people in abject submis-
sion to the wishes of their pro-slavery rulers.
After this concession to unrepentant rebels, it
would not be at all surprising to hear that the
National troops were to be removed from those
States, where their presence is the only security
the freedmen have from outrage and tyranny.
The troops once withdrawn from the rebel States,
a system of persecution and tyranny will be
organized against the coloured people. Once the
war power is laid down and State Governments

inaugurated, what is to prevent the Southern whites from enacting laws by which the freedmen will have as little protection for life, liberty, and property—as little control of their own actions—in fact, from making them slaves in all but the name? To bring about this condition it will not even be necessary to enact new laws; the brutal slave-codes of the rebel States will answer every purpose. Under these codes no coloured person's testimony can be taken against a white person. Even were these codes abrogated, nothing more would be needed than the prejudice that exists in the courts of justice in the South. If the Southern States are allowed to reorganize and assume their former position in the Union, without granting the negro suffrage and perfect equality before the law, the poor black man will be left to the tender mercies of the slaveholders, who will take a fiendish pleasure in wreaking vengeance upon him for his fidelity and loyalty to the Government. And to this condition is the policy of Mr. Johnson tending.

The white population of the Slave States have been corrupted by vicious institutions, which have rendered them totally unfit to participate in the reconstruction of the Southern States on a basis of freedom and equality; and if the

14

power of legislation is given to this class alone,
the natural consequence will be, that the
coloured people, who are the only loyal people
in the South, will be deprived of the little
freedom which they now enjoy, and remanded
back into slavery.   The votes of the loyal black-
men are absolutely required to neutralize the
votes of black-hearted white men.   The Government should demand that the intelligent coloured
man should have an equal voice in the reconstruction of the Southern States.   Before these
States should be permitted to have a share in the
Government, they should be required to give a
guarantee to freedom, and that guarantee should
be the immediate levelling of every obstruction
they have placed in the path of the negro by
unjust and cruel enactments, and the extension
of the right of suffrage and complete equality
before the law.   This should be made the unalterable condition upon which alone they can be
permitted to regain their forfeited position.
Unless that condition is established and acted
upon, the Northern people stand a fair chance of
losing the fruits of their great conquest, and the
coloured people will be left to the cruel and vindictive passions of their former masters ; and the
extent to which their cruelty and cowardly brutality can extend, may be seen in the records of
the horrid prison pen at Andersonville, Georgia,

where 30,000 Union prisoners were systematically starved to death.

How long the patient and docile negro will bear the wrongs and injustice heaped upon him, we cannot tell ; but there is a limit to human patience, and the cruelties practised upon this innocent and long-suffering people, may yet result in a disastrous war of races.

October 1st, 1865.

———

RECONSTRUCTION OF THE SOUTHERN STATES.
(JULY 25, 1865.)

To a nation there can be no greater danger than the existence of a flagrant injustice in its midst, protected and sanctioned by those in authority.

When the American people began their national career, they made this declaration :—" We hold these truths to be self-evident—that all men are created equal ; and that they are endowed by their Creator with certain inalienable rights ; that among these are life, liberty, and the pursuit of happiness.   That, to secure these rights, Governments are instituted among men, deriving their just powers from the consent of the governed."   These great principles were solemnly enunciated by the founders of the Republic, and they appealed to the Supreme Judge of the world for the rectitude of their intentions; and, notwithstanding this solemn affirmation, the nation has proved recreant to these principles.   No wonder that Thomas Jefferson declared, in view of the national apostacy, "that he trembled for his country when he remembered that God was just, and that His justice could not sleep forever." Without repenting for the long oppression of the coloured race, and without evincing the least gratitude toward the negro for his aid and assistance in overthrowing the enemies of freedom, they basely determine to leave the coloured people in the power of their cruel oppressors.   Could there be greater baseness ?   Could there be blacker ingratitude ?

The President of the United States, in his proclamation appointing a Provisional Governor for Mississippi, announces that none are to be allowed to vote for members of the Convention (called to restore the State to the Union) but those who were qualified as voters in 1861 ; thus summarily depriving the loyal blacks of all voice in the reconstruction of the South, and placing the power directly into the hands of rebels yet red with the blood of Union men.

If the terrible scenes through which the American nation has passed during the last four years has not been sufficient to teach it its solemn duty to the oppressed people of the South, it may yet have to pass through a more fiery ordeal—a war of races. Well might Jefferson exclaim, in view of such an event, "The Almighty has no attribute that will not take sides with the oppressed against the oppressor." In the midst of their rejoicings over the collapse of the rebellion, the American people should not forget to deal justly with the coloured race. They need not expect the favour of Heaven, or a true and permanent peace until they level every obstruction, and give the freedman the right of suffrage, and place him in a position to freely enjoy those inalienable rights which the founders of the nation declared to be "self-evident truths." The logic of American institutions and the principles of the men who achieved their independence and framed those institutions should impel the American Government to this course, which is demanded alike by justice, humanity, and expediency. But if the inalienable rights of four millions of men are wickedly and unjustly ignored, their appeals for justice will not go forth in vain.

AMERICAN POLITICS, (MARCH 2, 1865).

While on a recent visit to the United States, I had many opportunities of conversing with intelligent Americans upon the all-absorbing question of Reconstruction, now the chief topic of conversation in the United States.

The conflict existing between the President and Congress, and the results that may arise from a continuance of that conflict, give much anxiety to loyal Americans. From the tone of the President's remarks and public speeches, soon after his accession to the Presidency, the loyal and liberty-loving people of the Union were led to believe that the President was in favour of re-establishing the foundation of the country upon the just and enduring basis of *equal rights to all;* but it soon became apparent that the President had a policy which was none other than the restoration of Southern rebels to all the rights they had forfeited by their wicked attempt to destroy the country.

The object the President has in view is quite evident: he desires to be re-elected, and, to carry his point, he has resorted to the tricks and wiles of a political demagogue. To aid him in his efforts, he has formed an aliance with men whose hands are red with the blood of the murdered Lincoln ; and to propitiate men who, for four years, have been engaged in murdering and starving Union men, he has hastened to pardon and restore to impenitent rebels all the rights of citizenship, without asking security for the future, or without demanding equal rights for loyal men in the South.

During the last Session of Congress it became manifest that the President was determined to force his policy upon the country ; but Congress took a noble stand in opposition to the recreant President, and have maintained their position throughout.

The American people will certainly support Congress in opposition to the President and his demagogic henchmen—Seward and Weed. The great majority of intelligent Americans are decidedly more radical in their views than Congress ; consequently there need be no fear or anxiety as to the issue of the present conflict between the political parties in the United States. The great Republican party will be fully supported by the people in the elections now being held for Congressmen. It is true that some weak-kneed Republicans have gone over to the

President ; but it is equally true that they are men of little influence, and that little they have lost by their treason.

The President has already commenced the wholesale removal from office of men appointed by Mr. Lincoln, and is filling their places with his time-serving friends and favorites of the Copperhead species.   As Mr. Johnson is a man of violent passions, strong will, and very unscrupulous, the question naturally arises, what will he do, in case he is defeated at the present elections ? One of his favorites, Montgomery Blair, declares the President's determination to be the inauguration of another civil war, if the loyal people return a Congress opposed to his policy.   If that is the President's determination, and he attempts to carry it out, he will speedily meet the punishment he merits.

THE BLACKS IN CANADA—THE LAWS—THE NEGRO FITTED TO ENJOY LIBERTY.

Letter to "New York Tribune," July 10, 1865.

There is a resident population of between 40,000 and 50,000 colored people in Canada, of which a large proportion were once held in cruel vassalage in the Southern States, and, after enduring innumerable perils, found a refuge in this Province from the wrongs and outrages heaped upon them by their wicked task-masters.

The laws of Canada make no distinction as to colour. The negro is placed upon equality with the emigrants from other countries, entitled to all the privileges, and eligible to office ; and, notwithstanding they have had to encounter many obstacles in a climate very different from that to which they have been accustomed, their prosperity equals that of any other people in our midst. They fully appreciate the benefits of education ; they are quiet, docile, industrious citizens—many of them have become wealthy, and some have attained to high positions in the learned professions.

There is very much foolish talk in the United States about "protecting the negro," and "fitting him to enjoy the blessings of liberty." From my experience of the colored people of Canada (and I have enjoyed unusual advantages that have enabled me to become familiar with their condition and properties), I believe them quite as capable of appreciating their freedom, and much more deserving of it, than thousands of white voters in the City of New York. The negro

needs no protection—no preparatory course of
training.   What he does need is to be placed in
a position to freely enjoy those "inalienable
rights," which the founders of your institutions
declared to be "self-evident truths."   It is your
duty to level every obstruction that you have
placed in their path, in the way of unjust and
cruel enactments, and, having done that, let them
alone to manage their own affairs in their own
way.

The logic of your institutions, and the principles of the great men who framed those institutions, should impel you to this course, which is
demanded alike by justice, humanity, and expediency.   But, if you continue to wickedly ignore
the rights of the coloured people, you may yet
have to pass through the fiery ordeal of a war of
races.

POSITION OF THE FREEDMEN IN THE SOUTH.
(JULY 5, 1865).

The basis upon which the seceding States are
allowed to return to the Union is being very
warmly discussed in the United States; and the
process of reconstruction is watched with the

deepest interest by Christian men throughout the world.

Anti-slavery and radical men demand that the freedmen of the South shall have the right of suffrage and complete equality before the laws, and maintain that the President has the constitutional power to guarantee these rights to the loyal coloured people of the States lately in insurrection.

On the other hand, there is a large and influential party in the Union who maintain opposite views, and insist that the question of suffrage and equality shall be left to the control of the white people of the States interested.

The Proclamation of Emancipation gave the negro parchment liberty, and the Constitutional amendment only secures that a man shall not be bought and sold, and shall have the right to walk in peace—nothing else. They have no other right that a white man is bound to respect; they cannot own land; they cannot testify in a court of justice. If a white man enters the house of a coloured man, and outrages his wife or daughter, he cannot go before the tribunals and claim justice. They cannot vote where the great questions that effect their destiny, their labour and property, are concerned.

And, if the question of suffrage and equality is to be left to the white men of Texas, Alabama, and Mississippi, beyond the reach of Northern influence, and outside the shelter of Northern law, the poor negro will, in all probability, remain the tool and victim of their former masters for many years.

I contend that the American people and Government are bound, by a solemn obligation of honour, to give the freedmen complete equality before the law, and the right of suffrage. In the hour of their direst necessity they called upon the negro for help, and tens of thousands of brave coloured men sprang to the rescue; and, by the aid they gave, the North succeeded in crushing the Slaveholders' Rebellion. Thousands of these negroes have shed their blood upon the battle field to maintain the integrity of the Union, and now, to remand them to the tender mercies of their former cruel masters, is worse than injustice—it is base ingratitude!

———

Why I Desire the Success of the North.
(April 5, 1865.)

I am frequently asked why I, a Canadian, so warmly sympathize with the Northern States in their efforts to crush the Slaveholders' Rebellion.

I reply: I desire the success of the North, because the Northern people are struggling to maintain the integrity of the Union, and prevent the building up of a slave empire on this continent.

I desire the success of the North, because it has espoused the cause of the poor down-trodden slaves of the South.

I desire the success of the North, because I believe the preservation of the Union to be essential to the progress of liberty throughout the world.

I desire the success of the North, because the ultimate release from bondage of four millions of slaves depends upon the overthrow of the Slave-holders' Rebellion.

If any further justification of my career were necessary, I might cite the attitude of Liberals all over the world. The Liberals among the public men of England, France, Italy, and Germany are in favor of the North. Cobden, Bright, and Mill, in England ; and, in Italy, Mazzini and Garibaldi, who will be known throughout all coming ages as the liberators of Italy, and the champions of universal freedom, are in favor of the North.

Finally, I am persuaded that however much my objects and motives may be slandered and impugned, that history will vindicate the course I have pursued and the position I have maintained since the outbreak of the Slaveholders' Rebellion.

RATIFICATION OF THE CONSTITUTIONAL AMENDMENT AND PROCLAMATION OF FREEDOM.

On the 18th of December, 1865, Secretary Seward officially announced to the world the glad tidings that the Constitutional Amendment abolishing slavery and involuntary servitude throughout the United States, or any place subject to their jurisdiction, as follows :—

To all *to whom these presents may come, Greeting:*

Know ye, That, whereas the Congress of the United States, on the 1st of February last, passed a resolution, which is in the words following, namely :

" A resolution submitting to the Legislatures of the several States a proposition to amend the Constitution of the United States."

" *Resolved,* By the Senate and House of Representatives of the United States of America in Congress assembled, two-thirds of both Houses concurring that the following article be proposed to the Legislatures of the several States as an Amendment to the Constitution of the United States, which, when ratified by three-fourths of said Legislatures, shall be valid to all intents and purposes as a part of said Constitution, namely :

" ' Article XIII.

" ' SECTION 1. Neither Slavery nor involuntary servitude, except as a punishment for crime, whereof the party shall have been duly convicted, shall exist within the United States, or any place subject to their jurisdiction.

" ' SECTION 2. Congress shall have power to enforce this article by appropriate legislation.' "

And whereas, It appears from official documents on file in this Department, that the Amendment to the Constitution of the United States proposed as aforesaid, has been ratified by the Legislatures of the States of Illinois, Rhode Island, Michigan, Maryland, New York, West Virginia, Maine, Kansas, Massachusetts, Pennsylvania, Virginia, Ohio, Missouri, Nevada, Indiana, Louisiana, Minnesota, Wisconsin, Vermont, Tennessee, Arkansas, Connecticut, New Hampshire. South Carolina, Alabama, North Carolina, and Georgia, in all 27 States.

And whereas, The whole number of States in the United States is 36.

And whereas, The before specially named States, whose Legislatures have ratified the said proposed Amendment, constitute three-fourths of the whole number of States in the United States ;

Now, therefore, be it known that I, William H. Seward, Secretary of State of the United States, by virtue and in pursuance of the second section of the act of Congress, approved the 20th of April, 1818, entitled "An Act to provide for the publication of the laws of the United States, and for other purposes," do hereby certify that the Amendment aforesaid has become valid to all intents and purposes as a part of the Constitution of the United States.

In testimony whereof, I have hereunto set my hand, and caused the seal of the Department of State to be affixed.

Done at the City of Washington, this 18th day of December, in the year of our Lord 1865, and of the Independence of the United States of America the 90th.

WM. H. SEWARD, Secretary of State.

Thus terminated the great struggle between Freedom and Slavery in the United States.

END.